PRAISE FOR *Football Faith*

"From the locker rooms of the smallest high school to those of the most powerful professional football teams, faith and football go hand in hand. I could have had my faith without football, but not football without my faith. Rob Maaddi has written an inspiring book that serves as a testimony of how faith motivates and substantiates athletes as they strive to overcome the challenges and humbly attain the triumphs."—TROY VINCENT, NFL Executive Vice President of Football Operations and five-time Pro Bowl cornerback

"*Football Faith* illustrates the true motivation behind many of today's athletes. No different than in life, we will be faced with many adverse circumstances, and these stories help to shed light on the faith and perseverance necessary to succeed on and off the field."—BRADY QUINN, NFL quarterback

"While it may be hard to tell how football and faith actually mix, it is easy to see that football players and faith can be a match made in heaven. When football players take the time to examine the spiritual—to see what God has for them through faith in Jesus Christ—then we have something. In this collection of first-person explanations of favorite Bible passages, we get a glimpse at how some of today's top football people interact with scripture. We see how they let God's Word guide their lives and inform their decisions. While these are not commentaries by Bible scholars, they are practical insights into how men in America's favorite game find hope, help, and encouragement through important Bible verses. *Football Faith* can help everyone who values the game and cherishes the Word to think through how scripture should be informing their lives as well."—DAVE BRANON, Former editor: *Sports Spectrum* magazine, Editor, writer: Zondervan's *Sports Devotional Bible,* Contributing writer: *Our Daily Bread,* Inductee: Cedarville University Athletic Hall of Fame

"Christianity isn't about religion; it's about having a relationship with Christ. Football Faith tells this story in an inspirational way."—MARK SANCHEZ, NFL quarterback

FOOTBALL *Faith*

52 NFL Stars Reflect on Their Faith

DEDICATION

For Jesus Christ, without whom I am nothing;
for my loving wife, Remy, and my twins,
Alexia and Melina, who are my everything;
and for my parents, Issa and Hayat, who made
me something. Special thanks to Tim DeMoss,
Pastor Mouris Yousef, Jason Avant, David Akers,
Troy Vincent, and James Thrash for inspiring
and encouraging me as I walk with the Lord.

Trust in the LORD with all your heart
and lean not on your own understanding;
in all your ways submit to him,
and he will make your paths straight.

PROVERBS 3:5–6

Winning the Game of Life

WHAT IS TRUE SUCCESS?

"What does it mean to win?" "What is true success?" My adult life has involved competition in two professional sports with over one hundred million fans between them, and almost any time I'm with a group of men, someone will ask one of these questions.

When I was the head coach of the Washington Redskins, we won three Super Bowls and four NFC championships. As the owner of Joe Gibbs Racing, my team has won three NASCAR Cup championships and over two hundred races so far. So, yes, I know a little bit about winning and success—whether it involves coaching fifty-three gifted athletes on an NFL playing field or leading over four hundred dedicated employees at Joe Gibbs Racing in Charlotte.

But you know what? I've got a lot of experience with losing, too. Make a questionable call that contributes to your team's defeat in front of ninety-one thousand screaming fans at FedEx Field in Washington— or on *Monday Night Football*—and you get up close and personal with the meaning of "the buck stops here." Watch a $200,000 hand-built Sprint Cup car dominate a five-hundred-mile race only to get "taken out" by an angry competitor just shy of the checkered flag—that's the textbook definition of losing.

Many of the most important lessons I've learned in my life have come not from winning but from failures and losses—not just in sports but in situations as a father, husband, and businessman.

What have I learned? For one thing, if you're living your life trying to be successful in the eyes of the world—the perfect job, lots of money, even fame—you're chasing a ghost and you'll never be content. Many of us get the wrong ideas about success and put our hope in temporary accomplishments. Our victories are short-lived. As an NFL coach, you're only as valuable as your last win; a championship ring might buy you a little more job security, but not much else. Racing is no different.

LIFE IS LIKE A GAME

So when guys ask me what it means to be a true success and what they have to do to win, I talk to them about life being like a game. You and I are the players. God is our head coach. You think He's going to put us on the playing field without a game plan? No. He's given us the perfect playbook—the Bible. Inside of it is the perfect play for every game situation you'll ever be in, from the kickoff to the final whistle. When I describe life as a game, I'm not implying that it's trivial; in fact, it is no ordinary game at all. The clock is ticking for you and me. When time's up and the game's over, we want to be on the winning team; eternity rests in the balance.

The fifty-two men whose stories you'll read in this book are committed to living their lives with eternity in mind. Empowered by God, they are looking beyond the competition on the field and toward a larger goal: following God's game plan for their lives as team players, as husbands, fathers, and sons, and using their influence to point others toward Him. Life is the most important game you will ever play, and if you're like me, you want to do what it takes to win. In my experience, when I've veered away from God's game plan, I've failed. When I've followed it, I've experienced victory—not always what I've imagined victory might look like—but success in God's eyes nevertheless. May you be inspired by these NFL players as you read their stories about how they're chasing the success that can only come from being God's man and following God's plan.

—Coach Joe Gibbs

CONTENTS

DAVID AKERS

And we know that in all things God works for the good of those who love him, who have been called according to his purpose.

ROMANS 8:28

I love this verse because it sums up two things: my part and God's part. We are to love God with all our hearts, souls, minds, and strength. He, in turn, guides us and works out the details of our lives for good. Loving God is not about doing "things." It's about having a relationship with Him and embracing the truth that God is looking out for our best interests—no matter what our present circumstances may look like.

God can do *all* things at *all* times for our good. I have witnessed this truth time and time again in my own life. No, life isn't a bed of roses. But I've learned that God can clean the weeds and cultivate this ground into His rose garden.

My goal as a Christian, then, is to live out the love of Christ to advance His kingdom. I want to be able to give God the glory in all the things that I do. How? By serving His children; by the way I live as a husband, father, and friend; by the way I give financially to His church and those in need; and by acknowledging His blessings no matter what my circumstances may look like.

That's why I like to focus on this verse each day: because it reminds me of God's presence and His promise that "in all things, God works for the good of those who love him."

DAVID AKERS

POSITION: Kicker

KICKED: Left

HEIGHT: 5 foot 10

NUMBER: 2

WEIGHT: 200 lbs

BORN: December 9, 1974, in Lexington, Kentucky

HIGH SCHOOL: Tates Creek

COLLEGE: Louisville

DRAFTED: Undrafted

HONORS: Six-time Pro Bowler; two-time first-team All-Pro

TEAMS: Washington Redskins 1998; Philadelphia Eagles 1999–2010; San Francisco 49ers 2011–12; Detroit Lions 2013

CAREER STATS

	Ranges					
G	0-19	20-29	30-39	40-49	50+	PTS
221	9-9	124-126	126-144	100-148	27-50	1721

Pat.				Field Goals			
XPM	XPA	%	FGM	FGA	%	LNG
563	570	98.8	386	477	80.9	63

Akers kicked a 63-yard field goal on September 9, 2012. This kick against the Green Bay Packers tied the record for the longest in NFL history and helped secure a victory for the San Francisco 49ers.

David Akers wasn't drafted by an NFL team after setting a school record with thirty-six field goals at Louisville. He was cut by three teams and was working as a waiter and substitute teacher before landing in Philadelphia and becoming one of the league's all-time greatest kickers. Akers played more games in an Eagles uniform than anyone ever (188) and became the franchise's all-time leading scorer (1,323 points). He was named to the Eagles Seventy-Fifth Anniversary All-Time Team, was voted as the kicker on the NFL 2000's All-Decade Team, and set the NFL mark for points in a decade (1,169 from 2000–2009). He holds several NFL records, including most consecutive postseason field goal conversions (19) and most field goals in a season (44) in 2011.

CORTEZ ALLEN

*Not that I have already obtained all this,
or have already arrived at my goal, but I press on
to take hold of that for which Christ Jesus took hold of me.*

PHILIPPIANS 3:12

I have this verse inscribed in my Citadel class ring. That's what you strive for at The Citadel—to get that ring. You put whatever engraving you want in it. I graduated in 2010, so it has a number ten on the front with this verse inscribed on the inside.

It speaks to me by saying that life is a journey, it's a process, and as long as you stay grounded and hold true to God's teaching and His truth, His Word, then you know it's possible. I try to live a life where I let Him direct my path. When I pray, when I ask Him things, when I talk to God, I just ask that His will be done so that I'm not selfish and I don't try to get selfish gain.

He keeps me peaceful, even in a game when things are going crazy. I say, "I give You all honor; these plays are for You." And that's what keeps me focused—that's what keeps me calm in games and keeps me on the right path.

Allen didn't play football in high school until his senior year. He ran on the track and field team.

CORTEZ ALLEN

POSITION: Cornerback

WEIGHT: 196 lbs

HEIGHT: 6 foot 1

NUMBER: 28

BORN: October 29, 1988, in Ocala, Florida

HIGH SCHOOL: North Marion

COLLEGE: The Citadel

DRAFTED: Fourth round (128th overall) by the Pittsburgh Steelers in 2011

HONORS: Two-time second-team All-Southern Conference

TEAMS: Pittsburgh Steelers 2011–

CAREER STATS

	Interceptions			Sacks	Tackles	Fumbles		
G	INT	IntTD	TOTAL	TOTAL	TOTAL	FRCD	REC	TD
55	6	0	0		135	3	2	0

A small-school standout at The Citadel, Cortez Allen developed into a playmaker by his second season with the Pittsburgh Steelers. Allen had two interceptions, forced three fumbles, and recovered one in limited action as a nickel cornerback. He became a starter the next year and scored his first touchdown on an interception return against Green Bay. Allen signed a multi-year contract in September 2014 and recorded interceptions in consecutive games that month before a thumb injury ended his season after eight games.

JARED ALLEN

My first goal in life and every day is to be a better man of God. Everything I have is because of Him. *Everything.* Jesus pursues people, but He also wants people to pursue Him. I took that to heart, and what I found was that the more I have pursued Christ, the more He has blessed me. I once learned at a team chapel that you can learn to handle anything if you walk the walk and live with integrity. I took that seriously and committed to watch my language and stop cussing.

That's what this verse talks about: your tongue can be the most evil part of your body. What you say can directly influence other people. So I started making little changes in my life, and not cussing was the start of that process. It's a small thing, I know; but I feel more peace in my life now when I close my eyes at night. And God's still working on me.

One other way I work on being the man God wants me to be is in reading my Bible. If I don't read my playbook, I'm not successful on the field. My Bible is my playbook for life. So if I don't read my Bible, how can I wear the full armor of Christ and stand firm against the world?

One thing I've learned is that when you think you're outnumbered, God has your back. He's always there with you. Football is what we do, but it's not who we are. It's our relationship with God that defines us. When I'm dead and gone, I want people to say that I was a great husband and father. When I die, I want God to say, "Welcome home, good and faithful servant." That's how I gear my life.

JARED ALLEN

POSITION: Defensive end

WEIGHT: 265 lbs

HEIGHT: 6 foot 6

NUMBER: 69

BORN: April 3, 1982, in Dallas, Texas

HIGH SCHOOL: Live Oak, Los Gatos

COLLEGE: Idaho State

DRAFTED: Fourth round (126th overall) by the Kansas City Chiefs in 2004

HONORS: Five-time Pro Bowl pick; four-time first-team All-Pro

TEAMS: Kansas City Chiefs 2004–07; Minnesota Vikings 2008–13; Chicago Bears 2014–

CAREER STATS

	Interceptions		Sacks	Tackles	Fumbles		
G	INT	IntTD	TOTAL	TOTAL	FRCD	REC	TD
172	5	1	134	479	1	3	1

Jared Allen has been one of the NFL's most dominant defensive players since entering the league in 2004. Allen has twice led the NFL in sacks, including a team record of twenty-two for the Minnesota Vikings in 2011. He had eight double-digit sack seasons, including seven in a row. Allen has had multiple sacks in thirty-five games, including one in the playoffs. Allen has even played on offense, catching two passes for touchdowns for the Chiefs. He was a finalist for Athletes in Action's Bart Starr Award in 2012.

NNAMDI ASOMUGHA

Let us not become weary in doing good, for at the proper time we will reap a harvest if we do not give up.

GALATIANS 6:9

I've loved this verse forever because it's a verse of inspiration. . . of not giving up. I think that's the story of my life. Most of the things I've accomplished, the victories I've achieved in my life, have come after failures. Over the years I've had many struggles in the process of getting to where I am. Whether it was school or playing Scrabble, nothing has ever come easy for some reason. No matter what the obstacle, however, when I would get upset and pray about it, for some reason I would always be led back to this verse. It keeps me going because I know at the end of the struggle there will be a reward if I remain faithful.

My career in the NFL didn't start well for me in my first two years. In my third year, things started to pick up. Through those first three years this verse was big for me, something that pushed me through. It was the verse I put underneath my signature at the end of my e-mails to always keep me mindful of it while I was waiting for my career to turn around. That's not to say that everything has turned or will turn out perfectly, but it is to say: "Don't give up and don't quit."

I've come to realize that I have to trust in my purpose and trust in my place. This verse helped me 100 percent during the two years I was with Philadelphia—when things didn't go as expected. I keep it in the forefront of my mind, try to stay in constant communication with God, and keep knowing and believing I'm in the right place. And Galatians 6:9 has confirmed over the past several years that I'm in the right place. . .no matter what happens.

Asomugha made his professional acting debut in 2008 and married actress Kerry Washington in 2013.

NNAMDI ASOMUGHA

POSITION: Cornerback

WEIGHT: 215 lbs

HEIGHT: 6 foot 3

NUMBER: 21

BORN: July 6, 1981, in Lafayette, Louisiana

HIGH SCHOOL: Nathaniel Narbonne

COLLEGE: California

DRAFTED: First round (31st overall) by the Oakland Raiders in 2003

HONORS: Three-time Pro Bowler; two-time first-team All-Pro

TEAMS: Oakland Raiders 2003–10; Philadelphia Eagles 2011–12; San Francisco 49ers 2013

CAREER STATS

	Interceptions		Sacks	Tackles	Fumbles	
G	INT	IntTD	TOTAL	TOTAL	FRCD	REC
157	15	1	2	356	2	1

Born to Nigerian Igbo parents, Nnamdi Asomugha has a Nigerian first name that means "Jesus Lives." Asomugha was one of the NFL's elite cover cornerbacks for most of the 2000s. He was considered a shutdown cornerback rarely even tested by opposing quarterbacks. Over a three-year period from 2007 to 2009, quarterbacks threw just eighty-five passes at receivers Asomugha covered and completed just thirty-one. Asomugha started a foundation in 2006 to benefit underprivileged children, orphans, and widows in Nigeria and Africa. He joined former President Bill Clinton and actor Matthew McConaughey at the 2009 Meeting of Clinton Global Initiative University (CGI U) hosted by the University of Texas at Austin to discuss the importance of global service and student activism.

JASON AVANT

Pride goes before destruction, a haughty spirit before a fall.

PROVERBS 16:18

Humility is all about recognizing yourself as being under God. If you are humble, you realize that you always have a Master, a Lord, a Creator above you. Therefore, you will place yourself in the right perspective and treat other people the right way. You will realize that being humble is knowing that God is everything and that you would be nothing without Him.

If God wasn't merciful, I wouldn't be here. He has granted me gifts and talents, and I'm His, so I don't go out and do whatever I want with the stuff He has given me. I don't need extravagant things, fancy cars, or whatever. Building your life on your own accomplishments is an avenue for becoming prideful. And that's a sin that God hates (Proverbs 8:13).

All of life is a blessing. How can I brag or boast when I didn't do anything to get the gift? I may have worked hard, but God gave me my abilities. It was His divine plan for me to be a player in the NFL. In the field of professional sports, athletes can get caught up in their own supposed greatness and then fall hard. You see athletes go broke, go to jail, end up dead. . . . But God hates arrogance because He has the power in life. But when a person humbles himself under God, that's what Jesus says His desire is for us.

EXTRA POINT

Avant hosts a Christ First Football Camp in Chicago and Camden, New Jersey.

JASON AVANT

POSITION: Wide receiver

WEIGHT: 210 lbs

HEIGHT: 6 foot

NUMBER: 81

BORN: April 20, 1983, in Chicago, Illinois

HIGH SCHOOL: Carver

COLLEGE: Michigan

DRAFTED: Fourth round (109th overall) by the Philadelphia Eagles in 2006

HONORS: Ed Block Courage Award winner 2010

TEAMS: Philadelphia Eagles 2006–13; Carolina Panthers 2014; Kansas City Chiefs 2014–

CAREER STATS

	Receiving			
G	REC	YDS	AVG	TD
132	15	3,999	12.1	13

Jason Avant overcame a troubled childhood and involvement with gangs to reach the NFL after an outstanding career at Michigan. He was a two-time candidate for the Fred Biletnikoff Award given to the NCAA's top receiver and led the Wolverines in several receiving categories as a senior. The Philadelphia Eagles drafted him to replace Terrell Owens. Avant is a sure-handed receiver known for his toughness playing in the slot and being an unselfish player who excelled at blocking downfield. Avant filled highlight reels with spectacular one-handed catches and emerged as a team leader and mentor for younger players during his time in Philadelphia. He left the Eagles after eight seasons and played for Carolina before reuniting with former Eagles coach, Andy Reid, in Kansas City.

MATT BARKLEY

I grew up in the church and went to a Christian school, so faith has always been a major part of my life. As much as football defines me in this world, it doesn't define me as a person.

I love playing football, but I'm not the best athlete on the field. God gives talents differently to different people, and He'll use those talents in different ways. God has placed me where I am and made me the person that I am in the position that I am. He's given me a platform to serve His kingdom.

I have always held on to this verse from Proverbs during my personal life, and it has aptly applied to my football life. After I committed to USC, I thought I had my sights set and my path was straight; then all of the sanctions happened. Our coach left, the university president left, the athletic director left. All of this forced me to trust in God because He was the one who made my path straight.

When I think of the trials in my life, I don't like to say, "God, why is this happening to me?" Because who am I to deserve anything? What have I done on this earth to compare to the majesty of God? So when bad things happen, it's very unfortunate, but I don't think we can ask, "Why me?" By nature, we are all sinners who are deserving of death; but by the grace of God, we are given life.

My faith is so important for me because it is the one certainty I have. First it was USC, then the NFL draft, and now the different situations I face in a game—in all of these areas, I have faced and will face uncertainty. But with my faith, I know there's a certainty that God is *always* faithful. He has been there. He is here. And He will always be here. It's so affirming to know that He is constant.

MATT BARKLEY

POSITION: Quarterback

THROWS: Right

HEIGHT: 6 foot

NUMBER: 2

WEIGHT: 227 lbs

BORN: September 8, 1990, in Newport Beach, California

HIGH SCHOOL: Mater Dei

COLLEGE: Southern California

DRAFTED: Fourth round (98th overall) by the Philadelphia Eagles in 2013

HONORS: Wuerffel Trophy 2010

TEAMS: Philadelphia Eagles 2013–

CAREER STATS

	Passing							Rushing			
G	COMP	ATT	%	YDS	TD	INT	RAT	ATT	YDS	TD	AVG
4	30	50	60.0	300	0	4	43.7	5	-2	0	.4

Matt Barkley finished his collegiate career at the University of Southern California as the Pac-12 Conference leader with 12,327 yards passing, 116 touchdown passes, and 1,001 pass completions. Barkley could have been a top-five pick in the NFL draft if he had left after his junior year, but he returned to school hoping to lead the Trojans to a national title and was the favorite to win the Heisman Trophy. Barkley and USC fell short of their goals that year, and he injured his shoulder in his final game. The injury caused Barkley to drop in the NFL draft, and he ended up as the number three quarterback in Philadelphia. Barkley saw action in three games his rookie year and appeared in one game in 2014.

BRANDON BOYKIN

Truly I tell you, if anyone says to this mountain, "Go, throw yourself into the sea," and does not doubt in their heart but believes that what they say will happen, it will be done for them. Therefore I tell you, whatever you ask for in prayer, believe that you have received it, and it will be yours.

MARK 11:23–24

This is a verse that I live by. It says to me that no matter what the goal, if you believe in God and have faith in Him and His miracles, you can do it because *all things* are possible.

I found this out firsthand when I broke my leg before the NFL scouting combine. When I wasn't able to work out or get ready, this verse really became my statement of faith and led me to where I am now. I had broken my leg in the Senior Bowl, so I had to have surgery and couldn't participate in my pro day or the scouting combine. I dropped from possibly being drafted in the first or second round to the fourth.

That's kind of my testimony: getting hurt and dropping in the draft but still ending up in a great situation. I started as the nickel cornerback as a rookie and didn't miss any playing time. Everything happens for a reason, so I knew this was God's plan for me; He wanted to put me with the Eagles. I've never really questioned what happened because this verse has been a part of me and has contributed to my growth as a person.

I've always had faith in God. Growing up, my parents instilled it in me. Sometimes that gets set aside in college; but as they say, you always come back to your roots. Leaving home, I always wanted to stay grounded in God and His Word. I knew where my blessings came from.

Now I wake up and read a scripture passage every day. My goal is to know the Bible in depth so that I know what I'm talking about when I talk to people about God and His Word.

BRANDON BOYKIN

POSITION: Cornerback

WEIGHT: 183 lbs

HEIGHT: 5 foot 9

NUMBER: 22

BORN: July 13, 1990, in Fayetteville, Georgia

HIGH SCHOOL: Fayette County

COLLEGE: Georgia

DRAFTED: Fourth round (123rd overall) by the Philadelphia Eagles in 2012

HONORS: 2011 Paul Hornung Award for most versatile player in college football; 2012 Outback Bowl MVP

TEAMS: Philadelphia Eagles 2012–

CAREER STATS

	Interceptions		Sacks	Tackles	Fumb		
G	INT	TD	TOTAL	TOTAL	FRCD	REC	TD
48	7	1	1	102	4	1	0

Punt				KO Ret			
TOTAL	YDS	AVG	TD	TOTAL	YDS	AVG	TD
1	7	7.0	0	54	1,242	23.0	0

Brandon Boykin was a dynamic and versatile player at Georgia, seeing action as a cornerback, punt and kick returner, running back, wildcat quarterback, a coverage man on both kickoff and punt teams, and at holder. He emerged as one of the NFL's top nickel cornerbacks in his second season. Boykin led the Eagles and finished second in the league with six interceptions in 2013. His interception of a pass by Kyle Orton sealed a victory over Dallas in the final game that season and helped the Eagles clinch the NFC East title.

SAM BRADFORD

Be joyful in hope, patient in affliction, faithful in prayer.

ROMANS 12:12

During my first semester at Oklahoma, I learned about patience and perseverance. I really struggled with the Lord that year. I wasn't getting a chance to play. I was sitting on the bench. I was waking up at 5:00 a.m. to go to workouts. Every team I was on in every sport, I had always played. I had never sat the bench, so it was a totally new experience for me. So I kind of turned my back on the Lord. I thought, *Why are You doing this to me? Why are You putting me in this situation?*

But then I started attending meetings for the Fellowship of Christian Athletes. I got back into the routine of listening to someone giving a message about God. It opened my eyes, and I saw that God knew what He was doing. When I second-guessed Him, I thought He was going in the completely wrong direction. But He knew exactly what He was doing; He had a plan for me. He's had a plan my whole life. For me to not trust Him, it was just ridiculous. So, like this verse says, you have to be patient and persevere through hard times when you're really not sure what God's doing. You've got to learn to trust Him and know that He knows what He's doing.

I really don't see a reason why you wouldn't want to have a relationship with Jesus Christ. Not only was He the greatest person to ever walk the earth, but He's everything I want to strive for; He's everything that anyone should ever want to strive for. You look at the things that He did. Everyone who's on this earth was blessed because of Him. To come into this world and to deny Him the opportunity to have a relationship with you is like a slap in the face to our Lord and Savior.

EXTRA POINT

Bradford reads the story of David and Goliath before every game.

SAM BRADFORD

POSITION: Quarterback

THROWS: Right

HEIGHT: 6 foot 4

NUMBER: 8

WEIGHT: 236 lbs

BORN: November 8, 1987, in Oklahoma City, Oklahoma

HIGH SCHOOL: Putnam City North

COLLEGE: Oklahoma

DRAFTED: First round (1st overall) by the St. Louis Rams in 2010

HONORS: 2008 Heisman Trophy winner; 2008 Associated Press College Football Player of the Year; 2010 Associated Press NFL Offensive Rookie of the Year

TEAMS: St. Louis Rams 2010–14; Philadelphia Eagles 2015–

CAREER STATS

	Passing								Rushing			
G	COMP	ATT	%	YDS	TD	INT	RAT	ATT	YDS	TD	AVG
49	1,032	1,760	58.6	11,065	59	38	79.3	97	247	2	2.5

A record-setting quarterback at Oklahoma and only the second sophomore to win a Heisman Trophy, Sam Bradford left after his junior season and was the first overall choice in the 2010 NFL draft. He had an excellent rookie year for the St. Louis Rams, setting a few records along the way. Bradford established a rookie record for most consecutive passes without an interception at 169. He also completed 354 passes, breaking Peyton Manning's mark for most completions by a rookie quarterback. Bradford's promising career has been marred by injuries. He was off to an excellent start in 2013 with fourteen touchdown passes in the first seven games but tore the anterior cruciate ligament in his left knee in week seven. Bradford missed the rest of the season and recovered nicely after surgery on his knee. However, he suffered the same injury to the same knee in the third preseason game in 2014 and missed the entire season.

DREW BREES

What good is it, dear brothers and sisters, if you say you have faith but don't show it by your actions? Can that kind of faith save anyone?

JAMES 2:14 NLT

I accepted Jesus Christ into my heart on my seventeenth birthday, on January 15, 1996. I walked into church that Sunday on crutches after having knee surgery my junior year in high school. Before that, I had gone to church with my family, but I didn't fully understand it or accept it. But it was at that moment on that day that I remember the pastor talking about God "looking for a few good men." All of a sudden the light bulb went on in my head and I thought, *Hey, that's me; I can be one of those few good men for God.* And for the first time, I really felt like God was speaking to me.

Being one of those good men means that you trust in the Lord, you trust that He has a plan for your life. You trust that He's never going to put anything in front of you that's too hard for you—so no matter what you face, you'll overcome it, and it will make you stronger. It's the ability to influence, in a positive way, so many other people, and just be able to spread the blessings that God has bestowed upon you.

When I had my shoulder injury in San Diego, I felt that was the worst thing that could have ever happened to me at the worst time. It was potentially a career-ending injury, and I started to feel sorry for myself. I started to ask God, "Why me? Why now?" I looked back after I'd already been in New Orleans a year, and I said, "You know what, God? That was probably the best thing that could've happened to me!" Otherwise, I would have never had the opportunity to be a part of this community, to be a part of the rebuilding effort after Hurricane Katrina. I feel like I'm a mentally tougher and stronger person for it: with my job as a professional football player, as a husband, as a father, and in my faith.

DREW BREES

POSITION: Quarterback

THROWS: Right

HEIGHT: 6 foot

NUMBER: 9

WEIGHT: 209 lbs

BORN: January 15, 1979, in Austin, Texas

HIGH SCHOOL: Westlake

COLLEGE: Purdue

DRAFTED: Second round (32nd overall) by the San Diego Chargers in 2001

HONORS: Eight-time Pro Bowl pick; one-time All-Pro; Associated Press Comeback Player of the Year 2004; Walter Payton Man of the Year 2006; two-time NFL Offensive Player of the Year; Super Bowl XLIV MVP

TEAMS: San Diego Chargers 2001–05; New Orleans Saints 2006–

CAREER STATS

	Passing							Rushing			
G	COMP	ATT	%	YDS	TD	INT	RAT	ATT	YDS	TD	AVG
202	4,937	7,458	66.2	56,033	396	194	95.4	360	247	13	1.9

Brees didn't play tackle football until high school and considered playing baseball in college before choosing football.

Drew Brees is widely regarded as one of the best passers in NFL history. He had a prolific career at Purdue where he set two NCAA records, thirteen Big Ten Conference records and nineteen school records. Brees holds numerous NFL records, including most consecutive games with at least one touchdown pass (54); highest completion percentage in a season (71.2); and most seasons with 5,000 yards passing (four). Brees left the San Diego Chargers after five seasons and led the New Orleans Saints to a Super Bowl victory over Peyton Manning and the Indianapolis Colts following the 2009 season. He finished the 2014 season with the fourth-most passing yards in NFL history behind Brett Favre, Peyton Manning, and Dan Marino and was fourth behind the same three quarterbacks for most touchdown passes.

CRIS CARTER

*Whoever is not with me is against me,
and whoever does not gather with me scatters.*

MATTHEW 12:30

I became a Christian in the spring of 1988, after my rookie year in the NFL. My teammates, Keith Byars and Reggie White, were instrumental in leading me to Christ. But truly inviting Christ into my life took several more years because I was still holding on to worldly things. It took me a while to realize that giving my life to Christ and being fully committed to Him are two different things.

My wife and I ultimately decided that there was a better life than what we were living. We knew Christ was the way. It was just a matter of submitting to His will instead of doing what we wanted to do. The hardest thing for me was realizing that, even though I was a great success in the game of football, I was really nothing without God. I never really had joy in my life. I had temporary happiness, but I was never really satisfied. My only satisfaction has come through a relationship with God. Choosing to follow Him was the best decision I've ever made.

I have a purpose in life, and it is to use the platform I have been given to glorify the name of God. God calls me to be truthful, to be frank, and to step out in faith. I'm committed to using my influence and my resources for His glory.

Like this verse says, you're either in or you're out. There is no in-between. You either love Him and want to submit to Him, or you're going to do your own thing. The one thing I always try to convey to people is they're either working for God or they're working for the enemy. And they have to realize that the sooner they get on God's team, the sooner they're going to have victory in life.

CRIS CARTER

POSITION: Wide receiver

WEIGHT: 202 lbs

HEIGHT: 6 foot 3

NUMBER: 80

BORN: November 25, 1965, in Troy, Ohio

HIGH SCHOOL: Middletown

COLLEGE: Ohio State

DRAFTED: Fourth round (3rd overall) by the Philadelphia Eagles in 1987 supplemental draft.

HONORS: Eight-time Pro Bowler; two-time first-team All-Pro; inducted into Pro Football Hall of Fame in 2013

TEAMS: Philadelphia Eagles 1987–89; Minnesota Vikings 1990–2001; Miami Dolphins 2002

CAREER STATS

	Receiving			
G	REC	YDS	AVG	TD
234	1,101	13,899	12.6	130

Cris Carter overcame personal troubles that led Philadelphia Eagles coach Buddy Ryan to release him in 1989, saying, "All he does is catch touchdowns." Carter turned his life around after going to Minnesota in 1990 and credits Ryan for giving him a second chance. Known for having great hands, running precise routes, and making acrobatic leaps, Carter left the Vikings as the franchise's all-time leader in many categories, including receptions, yards receiving, and touchdowns. He was the 1999 winner of the Walter Payton NFL Man of the Year Award for his outstanding community service. Carter is the only player selected in the supplemental draft to make it into the Hall of Fame.

JAMAR CHANEY

By the grace of God I am what I am, and his grace to me was not without effect. No, I worked harder than all of them— yet not I, but the grace of God that was with me.

1 CORINTHIANS 15:10

I got saved my sophomore year in college, but that doesn't mean I started living the way I was supposed to be living. I got hurt in 2008 and started learning more about God and following Him that summer. Then I ended up getting hurt again the first game of the season my senior year. I tore ligaments in my ankle and couldn't play the whole year. So during that whole time, I was a little down; but I figured that since I wasn't playing and was in rehab, I would just get closer and closer to God and that really helped me out. Before the injury, I was getting my mind-set right, and my roommate and I were holding each other accountable. But football can take up a lot of time; and when I got hurt, I just had more time to study the Word, meditate on it, memorize it, and apply it to my life.

Since that time I've come to understand that this verse means that God has blessed me with this opportunity to play football, so I have to do the best I can. . .go out there and play as hard as I can and put my best foot forward every day for Him. I give God all the credit for my ability to play, so I just go out there and do it for Him in the way I play. Whenever I get tired, I try to remember this verse and remember that God is in me, and He has blessed me to do what I do.

A lot of guys who play in the NFL don't realize that this lifestyle is short term. Even if a guy plays twelve years, he still has his whole life to live. I remember hearing Herm Edwards say, "Being a professional is an opportunity, not a career." If you look at your life this way and view whatever you do as an opportunity that God gave you, then you will go out there and give it all you've got as an act of thankfulness to Him.

Chaney ran a 40-yard dash in 4.54 seconds at the 2010 NFL Combine. It was the fastest time by a linebacker in that draft class.

JAMAR CHANEY

POSITION: Linebacker

WEIGHT: 242 lbs

HEIGHT: 6 foot 1

NUMBER: 51

BORN: October 11, 1986, in Fort Pierce, Florida

HIGH SCHOOL: Centennial

COLLEGE: Mississippi State

DRAFTED: Seventh round (220th overall) by the Philadelphia Eagles in 2010

HONORS: Second-team All-SEC 2007; Defensive Player of the Game for the South in the 2010 Senior Bowl

TEAMS: Philadelphia Eagles 2010–12; Atlanta Falcons 2013; Oakland Raiders 2014

CAREER STATS

	Interceptions		Sacks	Tackles	Fumbles	
G	INT	IntTD	TOTAL	TOTAL	FRCD	REC
54	1	0	3	114	1	0

Jamar Chaney overcame a nasty injury—he tore ligaments in his ankle and broke his left fibula—in the season opener of the 2008 season at Mississippi State and returned to play as a fifth-year senior to improve his draft stock. He started two games for the Eagles as a rookie and made sixteen tackles in his first game. He started all sixteen games his second season and led the linebackers with three interceptions. Chaney was released by the Eagles after training camp in 2013, played one game for Atlanta that season, and spent 2014 with Oakland.

KURT COLEMAN

I keep my eyes always on the LORD.
With him at my right hand, I will not be shaken.

PSALM 16:8

We all go through difficult times in life, and when I do, I place my faith in God so I don't get rattled. People always ask me, "Why don't you get rattled?" But I'm just not that type of guy. I've come a long way, and I continue to grow. So whether I'm dealing with day-to-day issues or larger ones, like my dad getting cancer, I choose to lean on God.

I believe we are here for a purpose. God has put us here for that purpose, and the more I learn the Word and the older I grow, the more I understand that football is just a platform for me to serve His purpose. But I have to continue to build my relationship with Him to understand what that full purpose is.

God has blessed me with so many things in life, so for me to turn my back on Him would be a dishonor to Him and to myself, and I'm not going to do that. He's led me to a great place in life right now, and I'm excited to see where I'm going to go in the future.

Ultimately, life on earth is very short term, and life in heaven will be for an eternity. Knowing this gives me a mind-set to know that's what I'm working for, but first I have to fulfill what God has for me on earth so I can get there. I think people often get caught up with what the world offers as fun. But I don't want to be distracted by that. I find that doing my best to live by God's Word gives me more freedom to be who God really wants me to be. I find that my life is simplified and easier when I live by the Word.

While at Ohio State, Coleman was president of the school's chapter of Uplifting Athletes, an organization geared toward fund-raising efforts for rare diseases.

KURT COLEMAN

POSITION: Safety

WEIGHT: 195 lbs

HEIGHT: 5 foot 11

NUMBER: 42

BORN: July 1, 1988, in Clayton, Ohio

HIGH SCHOOL: Northmont

COLLEGE: Ohio State

DRAFTED: Seventh round (244th overall) by the Philadelphia Eagles in 2010

HONORS: First-team All-Big Ten 2009

TEAMS: Philadelphia Eagles 2010–13; Kansas City Chiefs 2014; Carolina Panthers 2015–

CAREER STATS

	Interceptions		Sacks	Tackles	Fumbles		
G	INT	IntTD	TOTAL	TOTAL	FRCD	REC	TD
74	10	0	0	191	3	1	0

A three-year starter and team captain at Ohio State, Kurt Coleman nearly quit football after an unfortunate accident at a spring practice when he tackled wide receiver Tyson Gentry and Gentry became paralyzed. Gentry forgave Coleman during a hospital visit. Coleman went from being a seventh-round pick to full-time starter by his second season with the Philadelphia Eagles. He became the eleventh player in Eagles history to intercept three passes in a game—against Washington's Rex Grossman on October 16, 2011. Coleman joined the Chiefs in 2014, started three games, and made three interceptions.

RANDALL CUNNINGHAM

For everything there is a season, a time for every activity under heaven. A time to be born and a time to die. A time to plant and a time to harvest. A time to kill and a time to heal. A time to tear down and a time to build up. A time to cry and a time to laugh. A time to grieve and a time to dance.

ECCLESIASTES 3:1–4 NLT

My last year playing in Philadelphia, I had so much anger inside for sitting the bench or for not being treated the way I thought I should be treated. Being the backup quarterback for the Eagles was difficult, but God allowed me to be patient and to persevere through it. No one really wants to be a benchwarmer, but there's a time and a place. This Bible verse says there's a time to mourn, a time to laugh, a time to weep, a time to cry—there's a time for everything, basically. There's a time to tear down, and there's a time to build up. That was my tearing-down time. I was humbled so God could rebuild me as a person, not just as a football player.

Each time I went to Bible study that year, it was like the Bible study was directed toward me—especially when we studied about submitting to the governing authorities. I learned there's no authority except that which God has instituted. So I had to follow the people God had put in charge. By doing that, God blessed me to go to Minnesota, have great success there, and be able to walk out where I could be thankful and satisfied for what He had done in my life.

Regardless of the situation, I have faith in Christ because He's the one who's going to pull me through the tough times. And when I'm going through the good times I'm going to give Him the glory, because that's what I've learned from reading the Word.

Cunningham's 91-yard punt against the New York Giants on December 3, 1989, is the longest in Eagles history and fourth longest in NFL history.

RANDALL CUNNINGHAM

POSITION: Quarterback   Throws: Right

HEIGHT: 6 foot 4   Number: 12

WEIGHT: 212 lbs

BORN: March 27, 1963, in Santa Barbara, California

HIGH SCHOOL: Santa Barbara

COLLEGE: UNLV

DRAFTED: Second round (37th overall) by the Philadelphia Eagles in 1985

HONORS: Four-time Pro Bowler; one-time first-team All-Pro; 1992 Associated Press NFL Comeback Player of the Year; three-time Bert Bell Award for NFL Player of the Year by the Maxwell Club

TEAMS: Philadelphia Eagles 1985–95; Minnesota Vikings 1997–99; Dallas Cowboys 2000; Baltimore Ravens 2001

CAREER STATS

	Passing							Rushing			
G	COMP	ATT	%	YDS	TD	INT	RAT	ATT	YDS	TD	AVG
161	2,429	4,289	56.6	29,979	207	134	81.5	775	4,928	35	6.4

Nicknamed the "Ultimate Weapon" by *Sports Illustrated*, Randall Cunningham was one of the NFL's greatest running quarterbacks. Gifted with a powerful arm, excellent speed, and the unique ability to escape pressure, Cunningham created nightmares for opposing defenses. He led the Eagles to three straight playoff appearances from 1988 to 1990. After missing fifteen games in 1992 following knee surgery, Cunningham returned to lead the Eagles to their first playoff victory in twelve years. Cunningham had his best season with the Vikings in 1998, leading them to a 15-1 record and finishing first in the NFL with a 106.0 passer rating. Cunningham finished his career with the most rushing yards by a quarterback (4,928) before he was surpassed by Michael Vick in 2011. Cunningham became an ordained minister after retiring.

BRIAN DAWKINS

Faith is important to me because it's the foundation for who I am. Everything that I am comes from my faith and my relationship with the Father. Being a patient man, a forgiving man, a loving man—all those things that you kind of take for granted—come from having my relationship right with my Father.

I know that everything I am and everything I need to become starts with my faith. Therefore, it's a constant humbling process because I know I'm not where I need to be, but I'm not where I used to be. I'm a work in progress, and understanding that has helped me grow through the years.

This verse tells me that if I find myself operating in fear, then I'm operating outside of the Spirit that God has given me. The gift of the Spirit in me is a gift of love. What type of love? That type of love that would give itself for me, the ultimate love that loves me *in spite of me*—the love that Jesus had when He died for my sin on the cross and rose again.

The Spirit has also given me power. What type of power? That endless power. The power that I can do all things through Him. There is nothing I cannot do with Him (see Mark 11:23–24).

Finally, the Spirit has given me self-discipline and a sound mind. That means I cannot make any excuses for the things that I do or don't do. I have the power within me to not do something that I'm not supposed to do. I can be strong in the face of fear, depression, or whatever challenge I face. Again, there are no excuses.

Dawkins became the first player in NFL history to have an interception, sack, forced fumble, and touchdown reception in the same game during the Eagles' 35–17 win over the Houston Texans on September 29, 2002.

BRIAN DAWKINS

POSITION: Safety

WEIGHT: 200 lbs

HEIGHT: 6 foot

NUMBER: 20

BORN: October 13, 1973, in Jacksonville, Florida

HIGH SCHOOL: William M. Raines

COLLEGE: Clemson

DRAFTED: Second round (61st overall) by the Philadelphia Eagles in 1996

HONORS: Nine-time Pro Bowler; four-time first-team All-Pro

TEAMS: Philadelphia Eagles 1996–2008; Denver Broncos 2009–11

CAREER STATS

	Interceptions		Sacks	Tackles	Fumbles			Receiving		
G	INT	IntTD	TOTAL	TOTAL	FRCD	REC	TD	REC	YDS	TD
224	37	2	26	911	36	19	0	1	57	1

Revered in Philadelphia for his hard-hitting style, passion, and intensity, Brian Dawkins is one of the most popular players to ever wear an Eagles uniform. He also was beloved by teammates and coaches. Dawkins was nicknamed "Weapon X," a code name of Marvel character Wolverine, the comic book superhero known for relentless aggression. He is one of only two players (Charles Tillman is the other) in NFL history to have thirty-five interceptions and thirty-five forced fumbles. Dawkins's departure from the Eagles following the 2008 season caused an uproar. Fans were angry that management allowed Dawkins to sign a free-agent contract with Denver rather than keeping him. He returned to Philadelphia in 2012 to become the ninth player in franchise history to have his number retired.

QUINTIN DEMPS

For the eyes of the Lord range throughout the earth to strengthen those whose hearts are fully committed to him. You have done a foolish thing, and from now on you will be at war.

2 CHRONICLES 16:9

This verse is inspirational to me because a lot of times I wrestle with whether God is even real, as I know a lot of people do. But this scripture opens my eyes to the fact that He is absolutely real because it says He's going "throughout the earth," meaning He's going from Asia. . .to Brazil. . .to the hood where I grew up to find somebody whose heart is loyal to Him, and then He shows Himself strong. He's looking for men who believe in their hearts that He's real.

People can praise God with their mouths and be all religious on the outside, but God is looking for hearts who really want to know Him. When He finds somebody like that, He shows Himself to be real. That's why this verse means so much to me. . .because if I am really seeking after God and my heart is really after Him, He's going to show me more than I can imagine. Once this was ministered to me and I got my heart right, He started to show me that He absolutely is real.

As NFL players, I wouldn't say we need God more than anybody else. True, our temptation level is a lot higher than most people because we are considered famous and wealthy, and when fame and wealth rise, so does temptation. That's the hardest part about being faithful to God. When you have money and on top of that you have power, you really have to be on your game and committed to your word.

That's the challenge for us. It's so easy to get worldly being in the NFL. But through the struggle, those of us who seek after God who want to be found faithful, need to stay rooted and grounded in a relationship with Jesus.

Demps started only two games in his five seasons with Philadelphia and Houston, and both came in the playoffs.

QUINTIN DEMPS

POSITION: Safety

WEIGHT: 203 lbs

HEIGHT: 6 foot

NUMBER: 35

BORN: June 29, 1985, in San Antonio, Texas

HIGH SCHOOL: Theodore Roosevelt

COLLEGE: Texas–El Paso

DRAFTED: Fourth round (117th overall) by the Philadelphia Eagles in 2008

HONORS: Two-time first-team All-Conference USA 2006–07

TEAMS: Philadelphia Eagles 2008–09; Houston Texans 2010–12; Kansas City Chiefs 2013; New York Giants 2014

CAREER STATS

	Interceptions		Sacks	Tackles	Fumbles			KO Ret			
G	INT	TD	TOTAL	TOTAL	FRCD	REC	TD	TOTAL	YDS	AVG	TD
80	11	0	1	119	2	1	0	108	2,855	26.7	2

A star safety at UTEP where he had a pair of 100-yard interception returns, Quintin Demps made his mark as a rookie kick return with the Philadelphia Eagles. He had a 100-yard kickoff return against Baltimore in week thirteen of the 2008 season and finished fourth in the NFL in kick return yards that year. He also had one sack. Demps played mostly on special teams before cracking the starting lineup in Kansas City in 2013. He also had a 95-yard kick return for a touchdown for the Chiefs that season. Demps signed a free-agent contract with the New York Giants in 2014, started nine games, and had four interceptions.

TONY DUNGY

*What good will it be for someone to gain the
whole world, yet forfeit their soul?
Or what can anyone give in exchange for their soul?*

MATTHEW 16:26

In all my years in the NFL, I saw this happen often: guys would get caught up in following the world and didn't spend time developing a relationship with Jesus Christ. When I was coaching, I wanted my players to leave me as better men than when they came to the team. My thought was that if they came to play for me, won a lot of games, made a ton of money, but they didn't leave as better people, then I hadn't done my job. That was my philosophy as a coach. Winning is what we got paid for, but I considered my job to be much more than that.

I told my players, "Don't put this game first. Don't make football everything in your life. How we relate to each other, how we live our lives, what you have in your heart, how you respond to the Lord, that's the most important thing."

After we won the Super Bowl in Indianapolis, we didn't start the celebration immediately. Instead, we finished with a team prayer on the field. I was so proud of the guys for wanting to honor the Lord in the victory. It was a great tribute for the team as they put the Lord first on football's biggest and most visible stage at the Super Bowl.

If people didn't know me and only knew my public persona, what I'd want them to know is everything that I do I do for the glory of the Lord. Because of my Christian faith, that's who I am. I wasn't always this way, but I'm very grateful that I am now. Certainly, I have ups and downs. I have negative thoughts, negative actions. When I was a coach, I didn't win every game. I have the same issues that everybody else has. But what I've tried to do is live by faith in my job and let my faith direct me in my life.

TONY DUNGY

HEAD COACH TEAMS: Tampa Bay Buccaneers 1996–2001; Indianapolis Colts 2002–08

PLAYER POSITION: Defensive back/quarterback

HEIGHT: 6 foot   **WEIGHT**: 188 lbs

NUMBER: 21

BORN: October 6, 1955, in Jackson, Mississippi

HIGH SCHOOL: Parkside

COLLEGE: Minnesota

DRAFTED: Signed as a rookie free agent by the Pittsburgh Steelers in 1976

HONORS: Two-time Super Bowl champion

TEAMS: Pittsburgh Steelers 1977–78; San Francisco 49ers 1979

COACHING RECORD

Regular Season		Playoffs	
WINS	LOSSES	WINS	LOSSES
139	69	9	10

CAREER STATS

	Interceptions	Tackles	Fumbles		Passing			
G	INT	TOTAL	FRCD	REC	ATT	COMP	YDS	INT
45	9	9	2	4	8	3	43	2

Dungy is the only player since the AFL-NFL merger to throw an interception and have an interception in the same game—against the Houston Oilers on October 9, 1977.

A standout quarterback in college, Tony Dungy mostly played defensive back in the NFL and led the Pittsburgh Steelers with six interceptions in 1978. After playing only three seasons, he began his coaching career as a defensive back coach for the Steelers in 1981 and became known as a defensive mastermind in fifteen seasons as an assistant. He was hired to rebuild the Tampa Bay Buccaneers in 1996 and guided them to four playoff appearances in six seasons before going to the Indianapolis Colts in 2002. He coached the Colts to a Super Bowl victory over the Chicago Bears in his fifth season with the team in 2006. Dungy was the first NFL head coach to defeat all thirty-two NFL teams. He was also the youngest assistant coach at age twenty-five and the youngest coordinator at age twenty-eight in NFL history. Dungy was the first African American head coach to win the Super Bowl. He joined NBC as a football analyst after retiring from coaching.

NICK FOLES

*Humble yourselves, therefore, under God's
mighty hand, that he may lift you up in due time.*

1 PETER 5:6

I started reading the Bible at a young age, and this verse has always stuck with me.

My parents raised me to stay humble no matter what—in good times and in bad times. They taught me to spread the credit to others when I'm doing well. Obviously, my teammates are the reason the team is successful.

It's hard to explain to others, but this is a verse that's very meaningful to me and it's one I have always gone to. It's very important to stay humble. As a young kid, I was always looking at the way athletes carried themselves, and my favorites were the guys who carried themselves in a humble way.

Now that I'm fortunate enough to be in the NFL, I have an opportunity to be one of those athletes to show kids who I am as a person, how my parents raised me, what I believe in, and how I go about my everyday life. My goal is to be and to always stay humble, to always be gracious, and to always be thankful for everything I have. . .because we never know what's going to happen tomorrow.

I pray every day, all throughout the day. Even in games, I'm praying. I read my Bible whenever I have an opportunity, whether I'm in the sauna warming up or cooling down after practice. In the morning when I wake up, I listen to Christian gospel music. I just continually think about scripture, about God, and keep my mind there. And I find that every day there's something new, something to learn. I find that the more I read scripture, the more I learn how to handle things better and be more disciplined. That's why I keep this verse in mind.

Reading the Bible is Foles' pregame ritual.

NICK FOLES

POSITION: Quarterback

THROWS: Right

HEIGHT: 6 foot 5

NUMBER: 9

WEIGHT: 244 lbs

BORN: January 20, 1989, in Austin, Texas

HIGH SCHOOL: Westlake

COLLEGE: Arizona

DRAFTED: Third round (88th overall) by the Philadelphia Eagles in 2012

HONORS: One-time Pro Bowler; 2013 Pro Bowl Offensive MVP

TEAMS: Philadelphia Eagles 2012–14; St. Louis Rams 2015–

CAREER STATS

	Passing							Rushing			
G	COMP	ATT	%	YDS	TD	INT	RAT	ATT	YDS	TD	AVG
28	550	893	61.6	6,753	46	17	94.2	84	331	4	3.9

After setting school records for yards passing (10,011), touchdowns (67), attempts (1,369), and completions (933) at Arizona, Nick Foles set Eagles rookie records in yards (1,699), attempts (265), and completions (161) in 2012. He then put together one of the greatest statistical seasons in league history in his second year in the NFL. Foles threw twenty-seven touchdown passes and only two interceptions in 2013, setting a league record for best touchdown/interception ratio. His passer rating of 119.2 was the third highest ever. He also became the youngest player to throw a record-tying seven touchdown passes in a game against Oakland on November 3, 2013. Foles broke a team record with 239 passes without an interception and led the Eagles to the NFC East title a year after they finished in last place. Foles helped the Eagles to a 6–2 start in 2014 before suffering a broken clavicle from a sack in a game at Houston on November 2, 2014.

KHASEEM GREENE

Even though I walk through the darkest valley,
I will fear no evil, for you are with me;
your rod and your staff, they comfort me.

PSALM 23:4

This verse is symbolic of a lot of the things that I went through in my life and a lot of the things that my grandparents taught me as a kid. I was brought up to know that when the dark days come, when difficult challenges arise, you know you have God on your side and you have Jesus Christ to guide you through it. Although bad days and sin are part of life, the relationship you have with God allows you to live your life to honor Him and to try to praise Him and bring glory to His name.

Although at times we don't think about God's presence and others don't believe it, there is a Higher Power who has already written the book on our lives; He knows what's going on and what we're going to do. Our role is to live our lives in line with that plan.

Believing in the Word of God helps us to remember that God is the one who has made everything happen, and He's in control of everything in our lives. That's what has helped me through the hard times.

Greene changed his uniform number from 59 to 52 in honor of former Rutgers teammate Eric LeGrand, who became paralyzed during a game in 2010.

KHASEEM GREEN

POSITION: Outside linebacker

WEIGHT: 241 lbs

HEIGHT: 6 foot 1

NUMBER: 52

BORN: February 4, 1989, in Elizabeth, New Jersey

HIGH SCHOOL: Avon Old Farms Prep

COLLEGE: Rutgers

DRAFTED: Fourth round (117th overall) by the Chicago Bears in 2013

HONORS: First-team All-American 2012; Big East Defensive Player of the Year 2012

TEAMS: Chicago Bears 2013–

CAREER STATS

	Interceptions		Sacks	Tackles	Fumbles		
G	INT	TD	TOTAL	TOTAL	FRCD	REC	TD
25	1	0	0	35	1	0	0

After switching from safety to linebacker as a junior at Rutgers, Khaseem Greene became a semifinalist his senior year for the Chuck Bednarik Award, given to the best defensive player in college. He finished his career at Rutgers with an NCAA record fifteen forced fumbles. Greene made his first career NFL interception against Minnesota on December 1, 2013, and returned it 49 yards.

MARK HERZLICH

*Even to your old age and gray hairs I am he,
I am he who will sustain you. I have made you and I
will carry you; I will sustain you and I will rescue you.*

ISAIAH 46:4

[Editor's note: Mark Herzlich was diagnosed with bone cancer in 2009 while a player at Boston College. After treatment, he went on to complete his senior season and play in the NFL.]

This verse is the one thing that stayed with me when I was going through cancer. When I was fighting that battle, it was so hard to do everything alone. It was one of the few times in my life when I felt totally helpless. When I was lying in bed alone, scared of chemotherapy the next day or scared of dying, that's when I would lose all control and start praying. That's when I felt God picking me up and carrying me along through the journey.

As I was going through my battle with cancer, I got a call from a college football player named Walter Musgrove. He was a Division II player who had cancer and had come back to play. He was very inspiring. He told me one thing that really stuck with me: he said to be very specific with your prayers.

I wasn't very good at praying because I didn't have a lot of practice. I was never a very religious person. I went to Sunday school when I was growing up, but on Sundays in my family we watched football. But I started to be more specific after that conversation. So every morning and every night while I was going through chemo, I prayed for two things: that I would get healthy and that I would play football again.

Because of the type of cancer that I had, the doctors told me that I would never be able to run again. But I truly believe in the power of prayer. I prayed every morning and every night for those two things specifically, and God made me whole again. The fact that I gave myself over to God in those trying times and let Him carry me through the last hard part of my journey definitely made my mind and my body right for me to be able to beat cancer.

Herzlich was the 2011 winner of the prestigious "Most Courageous Athlete" Award given by the Philadelphia Sports Writers' Association.

MARK HERZLICH

POSITION: Linebacker

WEIGHT: 250 lbs

HEIGHT: 6 foot 4

NUMBER: 58

BORN: September 1, 1987, in Wayne, Pennsylvania

HIGH SCHOOL: Conestoga

COLLEGE: Boston College

DRAFTED: Signed as rookie free agent by the New York Giants in 2011

HONORS: First-team All-American 2008; ACC Defensive Player of the Year 2008; Finalist for the Butkus Award for college football's top linebacker 2008

TEAMS: New York Giants 2011–

CAREER STATS

	Interceptions			Sacks	Tackles	Fumbles		
G	INT	IntTD	TOTAL	TOTAL	TOTAL	FRCD	REC	TD
58	0	0	0		97	0	1	0

Mark Herzlich overcame Ewing's Sarcoma, a rare form of bone cancer, while at Boston College and became an inspirational leader. He won the Rudy Award and the ACC's Brian Piccolo Award in 2010 after missing the entire 2009 season. He also earned the Disney Spirit Award, an honorary Lott Trophy, and the ACC Commissioner's Cup. Herzlich made his first career start during his rookie season with the Giants and earned a championship ring when New York beat the New England Patriots in the Super Bowl in February 2012. Herzlich worked his way into the starting lineup in 2014 and notched his first career sack on Philadelphia's Mark Sanchez in the final game of the regular season.

JAMES IHEDIGBO

Do not be anxious about anything,
but in every situation, by prayer and petition,
with thanksgiving, present your requests to God.

PHILIPPIANS 4:6

This verse is a constant reminder that anxiety and worry don't have a place in the Christian life. When we understand that God has our best interests at hand, He will open and close doors that will direct us toward His purposes. Now, worry is inevitable and human. People get in situations at different times in their lives and they worry about the outcome. But whether it's a financial problem, or a relationship or work issue, or anything else that's troubling, God tells us clearly in this verse that we shouldn't worry; but instead we should pray to Him and present our requests to Him and know in our hearts that He will provide the best outcome for us.

In terms of our dreams and our aspirations, if we have a relationship with God, we can continue to seek that closeness with Him so that we can grow into what He wants us to be.

Our team, the Ravens, went through a lot of adversity (in 2012); during the season, certain things happened that brought us closer to God as a whole team—coaches and players alike. When that happens, it's easy for people looking in from the outside to say, "Oh, they're just playing really well at the right time, and that's why they're winning." But those of us in the locker room knew better. We saw the hand of God on this team and felt His glory reigning on all of us. It was a special time and a great year.

EXTRA POINT Ihedigbo, the son of Nigerian immigrants, founded the HOPE Africa Foundation in 2008 to help provide educational services for underprivileged communities in Africa.

JAMES IHEDIGBO

POSITION: Safety

WEIGHT: 202 lbs

HEIGHT: 6 foot 1

NUMBER: 32

BORN: December 3, 1983, in Northampton, Massachusetts

HIGH SCHOOL: Amherst Regional

COLLEGE: Massachusetts

DRAFTED: Undrafted

HONORS: First-team All-Atlantic 10 2006; Division I-AA All-American 2006

TEAMS: New York Jets 2007–10; New England Patriots 2011; Baltimore Ravens 2012–13; Detroit Lions 2014–

CAREER STATS

	Interceptions		Sacks	Tackles	Fumbles		
G	INT	IntTD	TOTAL	TOTAL	FRCD	REC	TD
98	7	0	8	222	5	4	0

An undrafted rookie, James Ihedigbo developed into a valuable contributor for some of the AFC's top teams by playing well on special teams and in the secondary. He appeared in four straight conference championship games from 2009–12 and was a member of the Super Bowl champion Baltimore Ravens in 2012. He started every game at safety for the Ravens in 2013 and signed a free-agent contract with Detroit in 2014. Ihedigbo helped the Lions reach the playoffs and made a career-best four interceptions.

MICHAEL IRVIN

You intended to harm me, but God intended it all for good. He brought me to this position so I could save the lives of many people. No, don't be afraid. I will continue to take care of you and your children.

GENESIS 50:20–21 NLT

I turned my life over to Christ in early 2001 with help from Pastor T. D. Jakes and my friend and fellow believer, Deion Sanders. It took me forty years to really realize the hand that God had on me. I did almost every bad thing you could do, but it's through the power of God I can live this life. This Bible verse tells me what the devil will make for bad, God will make for good.

Sometimes we all have problems and they can get overwhelming, but when God saves us, we think about all He has brought us through and it's just amazing. You might say I should hide my problems, avoid talking about my past, but I just want to spread the word about how good Jesus is to me. It's His hand that brought me through all this. As Christians, I think we have a heavy responsibility to be witness to God's power. I know what God can do because of what He did for me. I don't want people to forget my story and rob God of all His glory.

Why can't you talk about God because you've made some mistakes? That's when you *should* talk about God. You go to God and say, "Help me with all of this." Spiritually, you use your falls to help improve your life and others' lives. You're not going to go through life without any faults. None of us is perfect. When you say, "I'm a spiritual man," you are saying, "I don't have the ability to live in the flesh. I have to live someplace else." Saying, "I'm spiritual" doesn't mean "I'm perfect." It means "I'm not perfect, and I need the help from God."

MICHAEL IRVIN

POSITION: Wide receiver

WEIGHT: 207 lbs

HEIGHT: 6 foot 2

NUMBER: 88

BORN: March 5, 1966, in Fort Lauderdale, Florida

HIGH SCHOOL: Saint Thomas Aquinas

COLLEGE: Miami (Florida)

DRAFTED: First round (11th overall) by the Dallas Cowboys in 1988

HONORS: Five-time Pro Bowler; one-time first-team All-Pro; inducted into Pro Football Hall of Fame in 2007

TEAMS: Dallas Cowboys 1988–99

CAREER STATS

	Receiving			
G	REC	YDS	AVG	TD
159	750	11,904	15.9	65

Nicknamed "the Playmaker," Irvin had an outstanding college career with the Miami Hurricanes, helping them win one national championship. He lived up to high expectations in Dallas, joining quarterback Troy Aikman and running back Emmitt Smith to form "the Triplets." The trio helped the Cowboys win three Super Bowl titles in the 1990s. Irvin was the team's vocal and emotional leader. A tough physical receiver, he was one of the NFL's most dominant players during this period. Irvin led the league with 1,523 yards receiving in 1991 and finished in the top five in receiving yards three times and in receptions four times. Irvin finished his career leading the Cowboys in every significant career receiving category. Irvin overcame many off-field struggles in his life to become a respected broadcaster and motivational speaker.

CHRIS JOHNSON

*"No weapon forged against you will prevail,
and you will refute every tongue that accuses you.
This is the heritage of the servants of the LORD,
and this is their vindication from me," declares the LORD.*

ISAIAH 54:17

This verse basically tells me that no matter what I come against in my life, God will always have my back; and no matter what I want to overcome, I can do it through Him. I always recite this verse before my feet even touch the floor in the morning. Why? Because throughout the day, sometimes I find myself struggling with negative thoughts. I find that once I start thinking like that, if I just keep repeating this verse, it will take all of those negative thoughts out of my mind. I keep reminding myself of this verse as I go about everything I do each day, even when I'm on the field. This verse is what keeps me going if I have a bad moment. Even if I only have a few minutes, if I think about it and pray, I can go and have a good rest of the day.

In 2012, as a team, whenever we had a bad game or we seemed to be down or in a slow period, I thought of this verse, and it just kept getting better for us. I really believe that our personal faith is a reason why our ride kept on going like it did as the season continued. We had Bible studies as a team every week that included our wives and any family member who wanted to come. We had many prayer warriors on the Ravens, and God truly blessed our team.

EXTRA POINT

Johnson scored a touchdown on a 99-yard kickoff return for the Rams in 2005 and scored on a 30-yard interception return for the Raiders in 2010.

CHRIS JOHNSON

POSITION: Cornerback

WEIGHT: 198 lbs

HEIGHT: 6 foot 1

NUMBER: 39

BORN: September 25, 1979, in Gladewater, Texas

HIGH SCHOOL: Pine Tree

COLLEGE: Louisville

DRAFTED: Seventh Round (245th overall) by the Green Bay Packers in 2003

HONORS: Super Bowl champion 2012

TEAMS: Green Bay Packers 2003–04; St. Louis Rams 2005; Kansas City Chiefs 2006; Oakland Raiders 2007–11; Baltimore Ravens 2012

CAREER STATS

	Interceptions		Sacks	Tackles	Fumbles		KO Ret			
G	INT	TD	TOTAL	TOTAL	FRCD	REC	TOTAL	YDS	AVG	TD
77	8	1	0	158	4	3	38	857	22.6	1

Johnson was a three-sport star in high school who also lettered in track and field. He played two seasons at Louisville after transferring from a junior college and intercepted a pass in the Liberty Bowl to help the Cardinals beat Brigham Young University. Johnson bounced around the NFL until finding a home with the Oakland Raiders. He started twenty-nine games in five seasons with the Raiders and had eight interceptions. Johnson left the Raiders during the 2011 season to care for his mother and his sister's children after his sister was killed by her ex-boyfriend and his mom was wounded. Johnson returned to the NFL the following season and was part of the Baltimore Ravens Super Bowl championship team in 2012.

ARTHUR JONES

I can do all this through him who gives me strength.

PHILIPPIANS 4:13

This verse means so much to me that it's tattooed on my body. It's a verse my brothers and I have grown up to believe in. With my father being a pastor, my family is built on strong faith. We have been through so much adversity that it's clear to us, and we firmly believe that *anything* is possible with God.

This verse has been a huge inspiration for me throughout my career; it's helped me all along the way in getting to this point of being in the National Football League. Starting off at Union-Endicott High School, my grades weren't good at all. I had a 1.7 grade point average going into my senior year. A lot of guys get distracted by sports and think they can be the next LeBron James or some other superstar, but I knew that without an education I couldn't move on. I went to summer school for two years in a row to get my GPA up to a 2.0 to even be able to take the test to get into college. Then I had to have faith in God that I would pass the test and get in.

Once I made it to the college level, I didn't play my first year at Syracuse. This required another level of faith—faith that God had put me in the right place and that I would get my chance.

I also had to overcome injuries: in my senior year, I tore my pectoral muscle and a meniscus in my knee. Although the experts were calling me a first-round draft pick, maybe even a top fifteen pick, I decided to leave it all in God's hands. I had to have faith in Him. I ended up being drafted in the fifth round by the Baltimore Ravens, and everything was amazing for me there. We won a lot of games, and I was put in a great situation.

Through this verse, I credit God with giving me the strength to make it to where I am today.

Jones is the older brother of UFC champion Jon Jones and NFL defensive end Chandler Jones.

ARTHUR JONES

POSITION: Defensive tackle

WEIGHT: 301 lbs

HEIGHT: 6 foot 3

NUMBER: 97

BORN: June 30, 1986, in Rochester, New York

HIGH SCHOOL: Union-Endicott

COLLEGE: Syracuse

DRAFTED: Fifth round (157th overall) by the Baltimore Ravens in 2010

HONORS: Two-time first-team All-Big East

TEAMS: Baltimore Ravens 2010–13; Indianapolis Colts 2014–

CAREER STATS

	Interceptions		Sacks	Tackles	Fumbles		
G	INT	IntTD	TOTAL	TOTAL	FRCD	REC	TD
55	0	0	10	84	2	0	0

Arthur Jones played sparingly in his first two seasons in the NFL before becoming a valuable contributor on the defensive line and helping the Ravens win the Super Bowl in 2010. Jones had 4.5 sacks during the regular season and got a key sack on Colin Kaepernick and recovered a fumble in the Super Bowl victory over San Francisco. Jones left the Ravens after four seasons and joined the Indianapolis Colts. Despite being slowed by injuries early in the season, Jones returned to the lineup late in the season as the Colts won the AFC South title.

COLIN KAEPERNICK

*You have armed me with strength for the battle;
you have subdued my enemies under my feet.*

PSALM 18:39 NLT

My faith is something that I lean on every day just to make sure I'm doing the right things. I've been very blessed to have the talent to play the game that I do and be successful at it. I think God guides me through every day, helps me take the right steps, and has helped me to get to where I'm at. When I step on the field, I always say a prayer, say I'm thankful to be able to wake up that morning and go out there and try to glorify the Lord with what I do on the field. I think if you go out and try to honor Him—no matter what you do on the field—you can be happy about what you did.

I know there were times during my first season in the NFL when I started questioning things, especially being my first year and not playing. I'd ask God what His plans were for me. What was He trying to do with me "right now"? There were times when I'd wonder if I was in the right place and in the right situation; and in times like those, I have to fall back on God and trust Him and know that His plan is perfect for me. Wherever you're at, whatever you're doing, that's what His plan is for you, and you have to make the best of it and keep moving forward. You have to keep striving, and things will work out.

That's why I love this verse. Basically it's saying that the Lord has given me all the tools to be successful, and I just have to go out there and do my part to uphold that.

EXTRA POINT

Kaepernick has multiple biblical tattoos, including the phrase "God Will Guide Me."

COLIN KAEPERNICK

POSITION: Quarterback

THROWS: Right

HEIGHT: 6 foot 4

NUMBER: 7

WEIGHT: 225 lbs

BORN: November 3, 1987, in Milwaukee, Wisconsin

HIGH SCHOOL: Turlock

COLLEGE: Nevada

DRAFTED: Second round (36th overall) by the San Francisco 49ers in 2011

HONORS: Two-time WAC Offensive Player of the Year

TEAMS: San Francisco 49ers 2011–

CAREER STATS

	Passing							Rushing			
G	COMP	ATT	%	YDS	TD	INT	RAT	ATT	YDS	TD	AVG
48	671	1,117	60.1	8,415	50	21	90.6	261	1,576	10	6.0

A talented and strong-armed baseball pitcher, Colin Kaepernick made the right decision to pursue the NFL instead. He is the only quarterback in the history of Division I FBS college football to have passed for over 10,000 yards and rushed for over 4,000 yards in a collegiate career. Kaepernick has emerged from a wildcat quarterback into one of the NFL's best dual threats. Kaepernick filled in for an injured Alex Smith during the 2012 season and led the San Francisco 49ers to the Super Bowl, a 34–31 loss to the Baltimore Ravens. Kaepernick set an NFL single-game record for most rushing yards by a quarterback with 181 in his first postseason start while leading the 49ers to a win over Green Bay. Kaepernick also took the 49ers back to the NFC title game in 2013.

BENNIE LOGAN

Trust in the LORD with all your heart and lean not on your own understanding; in all your ways submit to him, and he will make your paths straight.

PROVERBS 3:5–6

I grew up in the church, went to church all my life, and kept going through college. Playing in the NFL makes it hard to go to church on Sundays, so I make sure to do Bible study during the week. It's very important for me to read scripture and let it refresh me. You need that daily bread, especially when you have so much stuff going on. But you have to remember that God is there to help you and encourage you no matter what.

This is my favorite scripture because so many times things don't go your way in life; but if you just trust in God, lean not on your own understanding, and don't just look at the way things are going during that time when you're having difficulties, and trust Him, He will fix everything.

I was going through a situation my rookie year when I was not playing as much as I wanted to be playing. It was hard on me. Once I read this scripture again and cast all my cares on Him, things started to work out better for me. I just trusted that He would make it better, and He did. He made it even better than I thought it would be. I started letting Him lead me and guide me and direct me like He says in this verse. I just had to be patient and pray about it. I'm happy with the way everything worked out for me.

EXTRA POINT

Logan was the first player at Red River High School to have his jersey number (60) retired.

BENNIE LOGAN

POSITION: Defensive tackle

WEIGHT: 315 lbs

HEIGHT: 6 foot 2

NUMBER: 96

BORN: December 28, 1989, in Coushatta, Louisiana

HIGH SCHOOL: Red River

COLLEGE: Louisiana State University

DRAFTED: Third round (67th overall) by the Philadelphia Eagles in 2013

HONORS: First-team All-American 2012

TEAMS: Philadelphia Eagles 2013–

CAREER STATS

	Interceptions		Sacks	Tackles	Fumbles		
G	INT	IntTD	TOTAL	TOTAL	FRCD	REC	TD
32	0	0	2	69	1	1	0

Bennie Logan was not only a dominant defensive lineman at LSU, but he was known for being an unselfish player. He wore the prestigious No. 18 jersey during his senior year, a tradition at the school given to the player with the most selfless attitude. Logan was an immediate contributor in the NFL after the Philadelphia Eagles drafted him. He's a hard-nosed, run-stuffing tackle who became a centerpiece of the team's defensive line rotation.

CHRIS MARAGOS

*But seek first his kingdom and his righteousness,
and all these things will be given to you as well.*

MATTHEW 6:33

It's so easy for us to seek all of the things of the world and all of the things in our hearts first, but the Bible says to seek His kingdom first and His righteousness. Then secondly, *after* that, "all these things will be given to you." So often, people think *if I seek all these things, I can find the Lord in the midst of it*, but in reality, we have to seek Him first and then He'll take care of everything else.

I grew up in a Christian household. My brother is a pastor, and my parents are believers. I probably would've told you I was a believer back then. I knew a lot about who Jesus was, but I didn't know Him. I learned a lot of biblical principles at a young age that laid the foundation for my life, but growing up I idolized myself and I idolized sports because those were things that made me feel great. But when I got to high school and realized I wasn't the best player anymore and I was trying to find satisfaction from so many things that weren't fulfilling me, that's when the Lord took hold of me and saved me in my sophomore year of high school. It became real to me when I finally surrendered and gave everything up when I was fifteen.

EXTRA POINT

Maragos was a wide receiver at Western Michigan for two years while his brother, Troy, was Bucky Badger, the mascot at Wisconsin. Maragos used Facebook to tell Badgers wide receiver Luke Swann that he wanted to play there. Swann took his film to coaches, and Maragos was invited to play for the team as a walk-on.

CHRIS MARAGOS

POSITION: Safety

HEIGHT: 5 foot 10

WEIGHT: 200 lbs

NUMBER: 42

BORN: January 6, 1987, in Racine, Wisconsin

HIGH SCHOOL: William Horlick

COLLEGE: Wisconsin

DRAFTED: Undrafted

HONORS: Honorable Mention All-Big Ten 2009

TEAMS: San Francisco 49ers 2010; Seattle Seahawks 2011–13; Philadelphia Eagles 2014–

CAREER STATS

	Interceptions		Sacks	Tackles	Fumbles		
G	INT	IntTD	TOTAL	TOTAL	FRCD	REC	TD
62	0	0	0	39	1	2	0

After going undrafted, Chris Maragos has established himself as one of the NFL's top special teams performers. He played a key role on special teams for the Super Bowl champion Seattle Seahawks in 2013 and earned a three-year contract in free agency from the Philadelphia Eagles. Maragos made an immediate impact on special teams with the Eagles, scoring a touchdown on a blocked punt in his fifth game.

COLT MCCOY

"For I know the plans I have for you,"
declares the LORD, "plans to prosper you and
not to harm you, plans to give you hope and a future."

JEREMIAH 29:11

I grew up in the church with my family, born and raised going to church every Sunday morning and every Wednesday night. It was just a part of what we did. I gave my life to Christ when I was fourteen on July 8, 2000. That's why I'm here today. That's why I play, because God has given me so much ability. I think He's put me in this position to do good things and to be an example for Him.

Without faith, we are nothing, and without God in my life, I personally am nothing. Jesus was the greatest example that He gave us. Having faith in Him and what He did for us is awesome.

I think that if you're a Christian, you have the attitude of a servant; you have the attitude of a leader. If you can be an example, just like Jesus was on this earth, then people start to see the same thing, and it makes life a lot easier. There are a lot of struggles as a Christian. There are always decisions you have to make. I strive to make the right ones. I'm not perfect, and I've really had to trust in my faith and in my reliance on God to get me through.

Hard work, your teammates, your coaches. . .they will get you a long way, but without Christ you can't go the whole mile. That's what this verse teaches me.

EXTRA POINT

McCoy was a four-year starter in basketball in high school and was an all-state selection as a junior.

COLT MCCOY

POSITION: Quarterback

THROWS: Right

HEIGHT: 6 foot 2

NUMBER: 13

WEIGHT: 215 lbs

BORN: September 5, 1986, in Hobbs, New Mexico

HIGH SCHOOL: Jim Ned

COLLEGE: Texas

DRAFTED: Third round (85th overall) by the Cleveland Browns in 2010

HONORS: Maxwell Award, Davey O'Brien Award and Johnny Unitas Golden Arm Award in 2009; Big-12 Player of the Year

TEAMS: Cleveland Browns 2010–2012; San Francisco 49ers 2013; Washington Redskins 2014–

CAREER STATS

	Passing								Rushing			
G	COMP	ATT	%	YDS	TD	INT	RAT	ATT	YDS	TD	AVG
33	501	831	60.3	5,458	25	23	78.2	115	423	2	3.7

Colt McCoy was the runner-up for the Heisman Trophy in 2008 and left Texas as the winningest quarterback in NCAA history after going 45–8 and setting forty-seven school records. McCoy started eight games for the Browns as a rookie and set a franchise rookie record with a 60.8 completion percentage and 74.5 passer rating in 2010. He started thirteen games his second season, but Cleveland struggled to a 4–9 record in those games. McCoy was relegated to backup duties in 2012, spent a year in San Francisco and played for Washington in 2014. He started five games after Robert Griffin III was injured and led the last-place Redskins to a win on the road against the first-place Dallas Cowboys on *Monday Night Football*. McCoy finished the season with a career-best 71.09 completion percentage.

DAVID NELSON

What we do as professional football players is so highly publicized and criticized, it's easy to get caught up in what people say about you—whether it's the coaching staff, the media, or the fans. It's easy to lose sight of what the goal is, what the purpose is of your present circumstances, who you are really trying to please, and who you are really trying to impress.

For me, early on in my career, I got caught up in that. There were cameras everywhere; there was media everywhere. I wanted to please the coaches, and when I messed up, I got upset because I disappointed my coaches, I disappointed my teammates, and I disappointed the fans.

When I find myself distracted and moving back toward those feelings, I go back to this verse—because first of all, it tells me no matter what I do, I need to do it with all my heart and go at it with everything I have. That's who I am, and that's how I approach things. But then again, I'm not going to just do it. I'm going to do it for my Savior and Father.

We get so caught up in pleasing other people and trying to make other people happy that we lose sight of what our purpose is in that moment and who really gave us this opportunity and this platform. For me, this verse is a constant reminder to go out there and give everything I have not for people on earth, but to praise my heavenly Father who gave me these blessings and who gave me the opportunity to play in the NFL.

EXTRA POINT

Nelson caught Tebow's famous "Jump Pass" in the 2009 National Championship game to help Florida beat Oklahoma 21–14.

DAVID NELSON

POSITION: Wide receiver

WEIGHT: 217 lbs

HEIGHT: 6 foot 5

NUMBER: 86

BORN: November 7, 1986, in Wichita Falls, Texas

HIGH SCHOOL: S.H. Rider

COLLEGE: Florida

DRAFTED: Undrafted

HONORS: BCS National Champion 2007, 2009

TEAMS: Buffalo Bills 2010–12; Cleveland Browns 2013; New York Jets 2013–14

CAREER STATS

	Receiving			
G	REC	YDS	AVG	TD
50	138	1,530	11.1	10

David Nelson was a member of two National Championship teams while playing with Tim Tebow at Florida. Signed as an undrafted rookie free agent by the Buffalo Bills in 2010, Nelson had a breakout year in 2011. He caught sixty-one passes for 658 yards and five touchdowns. But Nelson suffered a knee injury in week one in 2012 and missed the rest of the season. He spent training camp with Cleveland in 2013, but ended up with the Jets after he was cut. He had a solid first season in New York, but was released after playing six games in 2014.

CHUCK PAGANO

To my mind, this verse speaks of how David acted when he faced Goliath. When David accepted Goliath's challenge (see 1 Samuel 17:8, 23), King Saul gave him some armor and a sword to use in the fight. But David told the king that he didn't want that armor; all he needed was a sling and a few small stones.

David didn't have a résumé that King Saul knew of, but David, even though he was young, had been doing this his entire life. In serving his father and protecting his sheep, David had killed many ferocious animals, including a lion and a bear. So he told Saul he had all that he needed to win the battle. That was it.

David wasn't timid; he was bold. I use this story and this verse as motivation in my own personal life, and I share it with my daughters.

The only reason I'm standing here today is because God is good. I'm very personal with my faith. Going through what I went through, fighting cancer, I just asked God over and over to heal me and I relied on my faith. After all, if you don't have faith and you don't have family, what do you have at the end of the day?

I couldn't think of a better way of making a living than coaching. I love what I do. But you go through what I went through, dealing with chemotherapy and cancer, it puts things in perspective. I know that eventually all of this (fame and fortune) is going to go away.

I don't think I ever took anything for granted. But now I know in an even deeper sense that it's a privilege to be where I am today. And I try to live my life in a way that reflects my gratitude.

EXTRA POINT

Two Colts cheerleaders and two dozen players shaved their heads in support of Pagano during his cancer treatment as part of a CHUCKSTRONG movement.

CHUCK PAGANO

HEAD COACH TEAMS: Indianapolis Colts 2012–

BORN: October 2, 1960, in Boulder, Colorado

COLLEGE: Wyoming

Chuck Pagano worked his way up from being a defensive assistant to getting the head job with the Indianapolis Colts. He guided the Colts to three straight eleven-win seasons in his first three years on the job, including two AFC South titles. Pagano missed twelve games his first year with the Colts after being diagnosed with cancer but returned to the sideline after three months of treatment. Pagano began his NFL coaching career as a secondary coach for the Cleveland Browns in 2001. He also coached defensive backs with the Oakland Raiders and served as a defensive coordinator for the Baltimore Ravens for one season before going to Indianapolis.

COACHING RECORD

Regular Season		Playoffs	
WINS	LOSSES	WINS	LOSSES
33	15	2	3

TROY POLAMALU

*Now faith is confidence in what we hope for
and assurance about what we do not see.*

HEBREWS 11:1

Football is part of my life but not life itself. Football doesn't define me. It's what I do and how I carry out my faith. Football gives me confirmation of how I can carry out my faith. It's my way to glorify God. I try to be passionate in every aspect of my life—how I love my wife, how I serve my children. In the same way, I try to serve my teammates and coaches with passion, and I try to serve God through football with passion.

People have this idea that the more pious and devout I am, the more successful I am, which is very dangerous. If you look at faith in that way, you're bound to fail at both—spiritually and in your career.

When I make the sign of the cross on the field, it goes back to this verse in Hebrews. Faith is confidence in what we hope for and assurance about what we do not see. So, when I make the sign of the cross before or after plays, I'm asking for God's support in those moments and in everything I do. It's knowing in your heart that God will take care of you, which might mean going head over heels into a situation having 1 percent for you and 99 percent against you. We all have to struggle to overcome our adversities, no matter how long we're in the desert.

Football, in general, has it backward. Players think this inner anger, this hatred, is what drives football and becomes the physical aspect of the game. But love overcomes all things. My love to glorify God through my playing will far outweigh anybody's hate for me.

EXTRA POINT Polamalu cut his hair (only a couple locks) for the first time in 12 years in 2013 to benefit the Veterans of Foreign Wars in a ceremonial haircut at Heinz Field on Veterans Day.

TROY POLAMALU

POSITION: Safety

WEIGHT: 213 lbs

HEIGHT: 5 foot 10

NUMBER: 43

BORN: April 19, 1981, in Santa Ana, California

HIGH SCHOOL: Douglas

COLLEGE: Southern California

DRAFTED: First round (16th overall) by the Pittsburgh Steelers in 2003

HONORS: Eight-time Pro Bowl pick; four-time All-Pro; Associated Press NFL Defensive Player of the Year 2010; NFL All-Decade Team 2000s

TEAMS: Pittsburgh Steelers 2003–

CAREER STATS

	Interceptions		Sacks	Tackles	Fumbles		
G	INT	IntTD	TOTAL	TOTAL	FRCD	REC	TD
158	32	3	12	576	14	7	2

After becoming the only safety selected in the first round of the NFL draft in the history of the Pittsburgh Steelers, Troy Polamalu became one of the best defensive players to play for a team known for its strong defenses. Polamalu helped revolutionize the safety position in the NFL, playing both the strong side and weak side spots and lining up at linebacker in a hybrid role. He has speed and quickness to cover receivers and is a ferocious hitter who is stout against the run and has a unique ability to sack quarterbacks on blitzes. Polamalu tied an NFL record for sacks by a safety with three in a game in 2005. Polamalu is a tough physical player who has overcome several injuries throughout his career. He helped the Steelers win two Super Bowls.

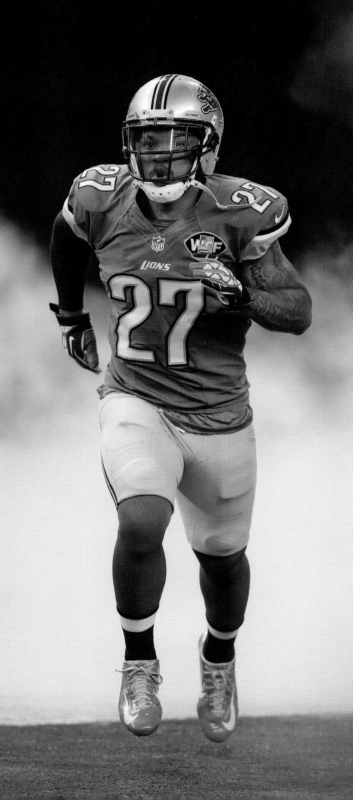

GLOVER QUIN

This is what the Lord says—your Redeemer, the Holy One of Israel: "I am the Lord your God, who teaches you what is best for you, who directs you in the way you should go."

ISAIAH 48:17

When I was at Southwest Mississippi Community College and I was going through the recruiting process, I didn't know where I was going to go afterward. I had broken my arm in the second game of my freshman year, and I had only played one season. During that time I remember the day my mom called me and told me to write this scripture down. She said, "Every day when you get up, before you do anything, you should read this scripture." So I listened. When I started quoting it and understanding more about God's Word, good things started happening and different things opened up for me.

What I get from this passage is that, in every situation that I go through, I trust that God is going to teach me to learn from it—whether it's a good situation or a bad situation. I trust that God will teach me to learn from it, to grow from it, and that He's going to lead me in the way I should go.

Sometimes I'm faced with difficult situations, but I trust that God will lead me to make the right decisions; and I trust that He's going to teach me to learn from them. I like this scripture because as an NFL player, meeting so many different people, it's hard to know who to trust and which way to go with everybody pulling me in so many different directions. So I just trust God's Word, that He will lead me and that He will show me the way to go.

I put everything in His hands. And it's worked out pretty well for me.

Quin was voted team MVP by his teammates at New Mexico in 2008. It was an honor that had not gone to a defensive back for the school since Brian Urlacher won it in 1999.

GLOVER QUIN

POSITION: Safety

WEIGHT: 201 lbs

HEIGHT: 5 foot 10

NUMBER: 27

BORN: January 15, 1986, in McComb, Mississippi

HIGH SCHOOL: North Pike

COLLEGE: New Mexico

DRAFTED: Fourth round (112th overall) by the Houston Texans in 2009

HONORS: First team All Mountain West Conference 2008; AFC Defensive Player of the Week, Week 12, 2010

TEAMS: Houston Texans 2009–12; Detroit Lions 2013–

CAREER STATS

	Interceptions		Sacks	Tackles	Fumbles		
G	INT	IntTD	TOTAL	TOTAL	FRCD	REC	TD
158	32	3	12	576	14	7	2

An MVP in basketball and football in high school, Glover Quin made the right choice by pursuing a career in the NFL. After a standout career at New Mexico, Quin stepped into the starting lineup his rookie season at cornerback for the Texans. He got his first three interceptions in the same game, setting a single-game franchise record against the Tennessee Titans on November 28, 2010. Quin moved to safety in 2011 and missed only two games in his career. After leading the Texans with seventy-one tackles in 2012, he signed a five-year contract with the Detroit Lions and led the NFL with seven interceptions in 2014.

BRADY QUINN

Consider it pure joy, my brothers and sisters, whenever you face trials of many kinds, because you know that the testing of your faith produces perseverance. Let perseverance finish its work so that you may be mature and complete, not lacking anything.

JAMES 1:2–4

I feel very blessed to not only be able to play the sport I love to play but also to use it as a platform to reflect my love for God who calls us to be a beacon of light as a witness to Him. As part of that effort, I've been signing my autograph with a variety of different Bible verses since I was a freshman at Notre Dame. I want people to look them up, hoping that if they read one scripture passage they'll want to read more.

This verse is a testament to my career in the NFL, but it means something different to everyone. No matter what our situation in life, everyone is going to face different trials. How we react is a result of our ability to persevere and rely on God to make us stronger. If we do that, in the end—when our journey is complete— hopefully we're not lacking anything.

Often when I pray, I ask myself, "Am I being the man today that Christ wants me to be?" Most of the time I say no because I feel I can always be more faithful to my calling. Hopefully when I'm older, when I'm seventy, eighty years old, I'll be able to ask myself that question and say yes with a pure heart and clear eyes. I'm just thankful that God is helping me, every day, to be the man He wants me to be.

EXTRA POINT

Quinn's 3rd and Goal Foundation grants "touchdowns" to qualified applicants that go toward building, or remodeling, homes/living areas for veterans and their families facing difficult living environments.

BRADY QUINN

POSITION: Quarterback

THROWS: Right

HEIGHT: 6 foot 4

NUMBER: 9

WEIGHT: 232 lbs

BORN: October 27, 1984, in Columbus, Ohio

HIGH SCHOOL: Coffman

COLLEGE: Notre Dame

DRAFTED: First round (22nd overall) by the Cleveland Browns in 2007

HONORS: 2005 winner of the Sammy Baugh Award for the NCAA's top passer; 2006 Johnny Unitas Golden Arm Award for the NCAA's outstanding senior quarterback; 2006 Maxwell Award for NCAA's outstanding player

TEAMS: Cleveland Browns 2007–09; Denver Broncos 2011; Kansas City Chiefs 2012; New York Jets 2012; St. Louis Rams 2013

CAREER STATS

	Passing								Rushing			
G	COMP	ATT	%	YDS	TD	INT	RAT	ATT	YDS	TD	AVG
24	296	550	53.8	3,043	12	17	64.4	44	185	1	4.2

Brady Quinn was a prolific passer at Notre Dame, setting thirty-six school records and twice finishing in the top five in voting for the Heisman Trophy. He started twenty games in the NFL and is best known for his eloquent comments after leading the Kansas City Chiefs to a victory one day after teammate Jovan Belcher committed a murder-suicide in 2012: "We live in a society of social networks, with Twitter pages and Facebook, and that's fine, but we have contact with our work associates, our family, our friends, and it seems like half the time we are more preoccupied with our phone and other things going on instead of the actual relationships that we have right in front of us." Quinn joined Fox Sports as an analyst in 2014.

PHILIP RIVERS

So let's not get tired of doing what is good. At just the right time we will reap a harvest of blessing if we don't give up.

GALATIANS 6:9 NLT

This verse is applicable to me in both my career as a player in the NFL and my everyday life. Through good and bad times in football, whether we win or lose, have a good season or a bad one, I can't get tired of living the life God wants me to live. Off the field, it's very much the same in my family life and in my everyday life. Through tough times or great times, don't get tired of being good and doing good things because we will all be rewarded in the end. There are also good times ahead for life here on earth.

We all stumble and fall. But it's never too late. You have to keep going. That's one of the beauties of reconciliation. I hold on tight to my faith, and the church, and my family. And that's when football seems to be at its best—when you have everything in the proper order.

No matter what the outcome of the game, I come home and I'm still a dad to my kids. And that's where it really settles in. As important and as much time as I put into football, my family thinks I did great no matter what.

That balance of the family at home, with our faith, teaching the kids the faith, having family prayer, going to services together, and then football, that's our role as dads. It's raising our kids in the faith. We always say a blessing at supper and pray with the family. Things they can hear and experience have long-lasting impact on them, and they can carry it into their families one day.

EXTRA POINT

Rivers started every game he played from seventh grade through high school and college, until his rookie year with the Chargers.

PHILIP RIVERS

POSITION: Quarterback

THROWS: Right

HEIGHT: 6 foot 5

NUMBER: 17

WEIGHT: 228 lbs

BORN: December 8, 1981, in Decatur, Alabama

HIGH SCHOOL: Athens

COLLEGE: North Carolina State

DRAFTED: First round (4th overall) by the New York Giants in 2004

HONORS: Five-time Pro Bowl pick; Associated Press Comeback Player of the Year 2013

TEAMS: San Diego Chargers 2004–

CAREER STATS

	Passing							Rushing			
G	COMP	ATT	%	YDS	TD	INT	RAT	ATT	YDS	TD	AVG
148	3,025	4,678	64.7	36,655	252	122	95.7	286	512	3	1.8

Philip Rivers led the San Diego Chargers to a 14-2 record in his first season as a starter in 2006, took them to the AFC Championship game in 2007, and has established himself as one of the NFL's most prolific passers in his career. Rivers set an NFL record for completion percentage (83 percent) for a quarterback who also threw for over 400 yards, tied a record for most consecutive games with 400 yards passing (2), and owns the record for most consecutive games with a passer rating above 120.0 with five. Rivers holds numerous Chargers records, including most career wins (88), most touchdown passes in a season (34), and highest career passer rating (95.7).

AARON RODGERS

I was fortunate enough to be raised in a Christian home, and my parents were role models who showed me what a God-centered life looks like. When our family had its ups and downs, I knew my parents relied on God for everything, and He always got us through those rough spots. So faith has been a big part of my life. In tough times I lean on Him, and in the good times as well.

When I was sixteen, Matt Hock was the leader of our church youth group called Young Life. Matt was the first person who showed me how much fun and how cool it can be to be a Christian. But I don't push my beliefs on people. I don't like to get in people's faces. The best way for me is this: let your actions talk about your beliefs. Start a relationship with others, then finally when there is a chance for questions, tell them about God.

My platform as a professional athlete and as the face of the franchise for the Green Bay Packers gives me a tangible way to share my heart and faith. In my daily life, walking in faith and dealing with life issues and not giving in to temptation can be very challenging. I'm always struggling to find time daily to grow in my faith. If you're not in the Word, or focusing on Christ, or into prayer, you can't help but slip at times.

But in those times, I recall this verse and remember the Lord is my Rock. He has always been there, always present at good times and bad; and to me, when I feel His presence, my life is full.

AARON RODGERS

POSITION: Quarterback

HEIGHT: 6 foot 2

WEIGHT: 223 lbs

BORN: December 2, 1983, in Chico, California

HIGH SCHOOL: Pleasant Valley

COLLEGE: California

DRAFTED: First round (24th overall) by the Green Bay Packers in 2005

HONORS: Four-time Pro Bowl pick; two-time All-Pro; two-time NFL MVP; Super Bowl XLV MVP

TEAMS: Green Bay Packers 2005–

THROWS: Right

NUMBER: 12

CAREER STATS

	Passing							Rushing			
G	COMP	ATT	%	YDS	TD	INT	RAT	ATT	YDS	TD	AVG
110	2,286	3,475	65.8	28,578	226	57	100.6	376	1,831	20	4.9

Aaron Rodgers replaced the legendary Brett Favre in Green Bay and led the Packers to a Super Bowl victory over Pittsburgh in his third year as a starter in 2010. Rodgers was the NFL MVP that season, helped the Packers win three playoff games on the road, and was MVP of the win over the Steelers. Rodgers has twice led the league in passer rating and he ranks first on the all-time list with a rating of 106.0. Rodgers has thrown for more than 4,000 yards five times and has a 70–33 record as a starter. Rodgers has the most consecutive seasons with a passer rating over 100.0 with six and he's one of only four quarterbacks to have a postseason passer rating of over 100. Rodgers also has the best touchdown-to-interception ratio in NFL history at 3.9 to 1. Rodgers holds numerous Packers records, including most passing yards in a season (4,643) and most touchdown passes in a season (45).

DEMECO RYANS

Trust in the Lord with all your heart and lean not on your own understanding; in all your ways submit to him, and he will make your paths straight. Do not be wise in your own eyes; fear the Lord and shun evil.

PROVERBS 3:5–7

This passage is essential to my faith in the Lord. Trusting in Him is how I'm able to make it through this day-to-day struggle of life. It is easy to trust in the Lord, knowing He always has my back, even when I stumble and screw things up. Playing a team sport like football, you have to rely on and trust your teammates to do their jobs. Unfortunately, everyone does not come through 100 percent of the time. As athletes, like all people, we stumble, make mistakes, and are at times unreliable because none of us live perfect lives.

I know the need of being able to count on the Lord when it seems that everyone is praising me and when I'm not the fan favorite. In this up-and-down world of professional football, I lean on the Lord for my understanding, which allows me to stay humble. When successes or failures present themselves, I can handle them both graciously, knowing that God is always directing every step in my life. I can praise Him when things go good or bad because I am His child, and He will always make my dark days bright.

Acknowledging God, through prayer and thanksgiving, and staying humble has allowed me to become a success in my profession. When others said I was not fast enough or big enough, God said I was just right. This passage is a constant reminder that I am nothing without the influence of God in my life. I pray that we can continue to seek counsel from God, revere Him, and not be too smart in our own eyes.

DEMECO RYANS

POSITION: Middle linebacker **WEIGHT**: 235 lbs

HEIGHT: 6 foot 1 **NUMBER**: 59

BORN: July 28, 1984, in Bessemer, Alabama

HIGH SCHOOL: Jess Lanier

COLLEGE: Alabama

DRAFTED: Second round (33rd overall) by the Houston Texans in 2006

HONORS: Two-time Pro Bowler; 2006 Associated Press NFL Defensive Rookie of the Year

TEAMS: Houston Texas 2006–11; Philadelphia Eagles 2012–

CAREER STATS

	Interceptions		Sacks	Tackles	Fumbles		
G	INT	IntTD	TOTAL	TOTAL	FRCD	REC	TD
126	13	0	6.5	703	6	9	1

DeMeco Ryans was a unanimous All-American at Alabama who quickly developed into an excellent, three-down linebacker in the NFL. He started immediately as a rookie for the Texans and had an outstanding season. Ryans went to his first Pro Bowl in 2007 and has started every game he's played in during his nine-year career. After being traded to the Eagles in 2012, Ryans quickly became a well-respected leader, on and off the field, known for his professionalism. He enjoyed a solid season in 2014 before suffering a torn Achilles tendon that forced him to miss the final eight games. Ryans overcame the same injury in 2010.

MARK SANCHEZ

When I think of Christianity, I think of the Ten Commandments and all the rules and what you can't do. But when I went to see Pastor Miles McPherson at The Rock Church in San Diego, this was the first verse he gave me, and his point was that it's all about your relationship with God. Christianity isn't about going to services or doing charity work. All that comes because you understand this verse.

If you love God, how do you show your love for Him? You can't send God flowers. You can't buy Him a car. There's no material thing you can give back. He's already done everything for you, so you obey. That's how you love God. So how do you love your neighbor? You help them love God. And you don't do it in a condescending way by telling them they're going to go to hell for doing something wrong. Just love them and be positive.

This verse changed the entire way I think of religion. Don't think religion; instead, think relationship. The most important thing is to ask yourself, "Am I loving God by loving my neighbor in everything I'm doing?" If you're going out with friends and you feel like having a drink, ask yourself, "Do I really need to? Is that loving God? Is that loving my neighbor? Is that helping my fellow Christian?"

I came to this realization in the 2013 offseason when I was going through all the rehab from shoulder surgery and looking for a new team. I wasn't a bad person in New York, but I wasn't the best version of me. I was having a lot of fun in the world, and it's easy to get caught up in that stuff when it's right there, when you win your first two seasons and you're on top of the world and you think it's never going to end. So when it started to happen in Philadelphia, I was ready for it. I knew why I was there. I have a platform. I can help people. I can do a lot to help.

MARK SANCHEZ

POSITION: Quarterback   **THROWS**: Right

HEIGHT: 6 foot 2   **NUMBER**: 3

WEIGHT: 225 lbs

BORN: November 11, 1986, in Long Beach, California

HIGH SCHOOL: Mission Viejo

COLLEGE: Southern California

DRAFTED: First round (5th overall) by the New York Jets in 2009

HONORS: 2009 Rose Bowl Offensive MVP; 2009 first-team All-Pac-10

TEAMS: New York Jets 2009–13; Philadelphia Eagles 2014–

CAREER STATS

	Passing							Rushing			
G	COMP	ATT	%	YDS	TD	INT	RAT	ATT	YDS	TD	AVG
71	1,226	2,176	56.3	14,510	82	80	74.1	159	429	13	2.7

Sanchez became fluent in Spanish by listening to instructional tapes on his commute to practice.

Mark Sanchez left USC early after an outstanding college career and led the New York Jets to the AFC championship game his first two seasons in the NFL. His nine touchdown passes in the postseason are the most in franchise history, and his 80-yard touchdown pass to Braylon Edwards in the 2010 AFC title game is the longest play in Jets' playoff history. Sanchez joined the Philadelphia Eagles in 2014 and set a franchise record with a 64.1 completion percentage in eight starts after replacing an injured Nick Foles. He threw for a career-best 374 yards in a loss to Washington on December 20, 2014, setting a franchise record with thirty-seven completions. Sanchez is one of four quarterbacks in Eagles' history to throw for 300 yards in three straight games.

DEION SANDERS

*Take delight in the LORD, and he
will give you your heart's desires.*

PSALM 37:4 NLT

Before I found Christ, I had all the material comforts and all the money and all the fame and popularity, but I had no peace. I had everything the world has to offer. I had everything that power, money, and sex could give me, but it just wasn't enough. It didn't satisfy me. I was empty inside—desperately empty. Success almost ruined my life, but thank God, I came to Him just in time. And that made all the difference.

When I found Christ, I found what I had been missing all those years. Only then was I able to trust in God's will for my life. I started having a new sense of peace about what happened on and off the field. I have a passionate hunger for the things of God, and each day I'm feeding on His Word.

I realize now that God had to get me to the point where He could do what He wanted to do with me, and that meant that first He had to strip me of all the comforts, all the success, and all the relationships I had depended on. Through the struggles and the doubts and the bitterness, He was bringing me to the point where I could see His hand in my life.

If you're not satisfied with what the world has to offer, you, too, can invite God into your life by praying, by telling Him you realize you are a sinner in need of a Savior, that you need and want forgiveness and a new life through Him. Take delight in Him, like it says in this verse, and He will give you everything.

DEION SANDERS

POSITION: Cornerback/
             Wide receiver

WEIGHT: 195 lbs

NUMBER: 21

HEIGHT: 6 foot 1

BORN: August 9, 1967, in Fort Myers, Florida

HIGH SCHOOL: North Fort Myers

COLLEGE: Florida State

DRAFTED: First round (5th overall) by the Atlanta Falcons in 1989

HONORS: Eight-time Pro Bowler; six-time first-team All-Pro; 1994 Associated Press NFL Defensive Player of the Year; inducted into Pro Football Hall of Fame in 2011

TEAMS: Atlanta Falcons 1989–93; San Francisco 49ers 1994; Dallas Cowboys 1995–99; Washington Redskins 2000; Baltimore Ravens 2004–05

CAREER STATS

	Interceptions			Sacks	Tackles	Fumb		
G	INT	TD	TOTAL	TOTAL	FRCD	REC	TD
188	53	9	1	492	10	13	1

Receiving				Punt				KO Ret			
REC	YDS	AVG	TD	TOTAL	YDS	AVG	TD	TOTAL	YDS	AVG	TD
212	784	13.1	3	212	2,199	10.4	6	155	3,523	22.7	3

EXTRA POINT

Sanders is one of only two players in NFL history (Bill Dudley is the other) to score a touchdown six different ways via interception return, punt return, kickoff return, receiving, rushing, and a fumble recovery.

Nicknamed "Prime Time" and "Neon Deion," Deion Sanders was one of the most electrifying playmakers and top cover cornerbacks in NFL history. He was a uniquely talented, two-way player in the NFL and two-sport star who also played nine seasons in Major League Baseball. He was a center fielder who had a .263 career batting average, 39 home runs, and 186 stolen bases in 641 career games with the Yankees, Braves, Reds, and Giants. In 1989, Sanders became the only person ever to hit a home run and score a touchdown in the same week. He remains the only player to play in a World Series and Super Bowl. Sanders works as an analyst and has made numerous other television appearances since his retirement.

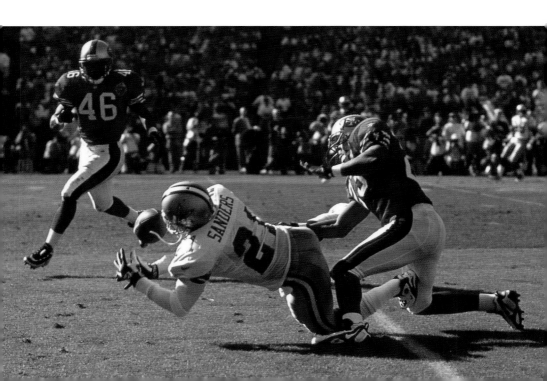

ROCKY SETO

For I determined to know nothing among you except Jesus Christ, and Him crucified.

1 CORINTHIANS 2:2 NASB

This verse has been haunting me the last couple years. Ultimately, as believers, that is the message of our lives. When it comes down to it, what are you about? Jesus. When I die someday, I hope my wife and my children say, "He loved Jesus—period. He constantly pastored us to love Jesus." If you're not consumed with who Jesus is, you're missing it. It's not about the rituals or semantics; it's about who your king is, and Jesus dominates me. In coaching, you coach excellence to build good relationships with players and other coaches, but ultimately you don't coach to coach and say, "Good job, see you next year." You have a great relationship, and when guys ask you what you're all about, you say Jesus.

Jesus is better than winning the Super Bowl. We had the blessing to win Rose Bowls when I was at USC, and when I woke up the next morning, I was the same person. It's easier when you win, of course. But when I became a believer at the University of Southern California in 1998, Jesus changed me forever. He changed my eternity, He changed my attitude, He changed my drive, and He changed everything from how I am as a parent to how I am as a husband. He consumes who I am. That's why Jesus is better than everything. Jesus is the greatest treasure any one of us can ever have.

ROCKY SETO

DEFENSIVE PASSING GAME COORDINATOR

TEAM: Seattle Seahawks 2010

BORN: March 12, 1976, in Los Angeles, California

HIGH SCHOOL: Arcadia

COLLEGE: Southern California

HONORS: Black Shirt Award for USC defensive player of the year 1998

Haruki Rocky Seto was a walk-on at USC and ended up being a valuable member of the scout team his final season. Seto immediately began his coaching career as a volunteer assistant at USC after graduation. He coached safeties, linebackers, and the secondary before he was promoted to defensive coordinator in 2009. Seto joined Pete Carroll's staff in Seattle in 2010 as the defensive passing game coordinator. He helped the secondary develop into one of the best units in the NFL during the Seahawks' Super Bowl championship season in 2013.

MIKE SINGLETARY

Love is patient and kind. Love is not jealous or boastful or proud or rude. It does not demand its own way. It is not irritable, and it keeps no record of being wronged. It does not rejoice about injustice but rejoices whenever the truth wins out. Love never gives up, never loses faith, is always hopeful, and endures through every circumstance. Prophecy and speaking in unknown language and special knowledge will become useless. But love will last forever!

1 Corinthians 13:4–8 NLT

I became a Christian for all the wrong reasons: fear of going to hell and the desire to make my mother happy. It wasn't until the first year of my marriage that I discovered this wasn't enough.

I had to come to a point of brokenness. The way I was going about things wasn't working. Football had defined me. I thought I was succeeding in life. The truth is, I wasn't paying enough attention to the most important thing of all—my wife and our kids.

I realized I couldn't be the great husband and man of God I wanted to be unless I started serving God for the right reasons— reasons that had less to do with my own needs and more to do with His will for my life. From that point onward, my life totally changed.

One night after a terrible argument with my wife, I sat in the den and reached for the Bible, thinking it would calm me. Flipping through the pages, I came across the love chapter in 1 Corinthians 13. Love is not boastful, not proud, not self-seeking. And it struck me: I was all of those things. I kept reading. But love never fails. Love is patient, love is kind. It is not easily angered. I read the verse to my wife and told her that she and the kids would be my top priority.

The Bible was so important to this change process. It's the Book of Life, the Ultimate Wisdom. If you sense the need for change, I encourage you to read the Bible.

MIKE SINGLETARY

POSITION: Middle linebacker **WEIGHT**: 230 lbs

HEIGHT: 6 foot **NUMBER**: 50

BORN: October 9, 1958, in Houston, Texas

HIGH SCHOOL: Evan E. Worthing

COLLEGE: Baylor

DRAFTED: Second round (38th overall) by the Chicago Bears in 1981

HONORS: Ten-time Pro Bowler; seven-time first-team All-Pro; two-time Associated Press NFL Defensive Player of the Year; 1990 Walter Payton NFL Man of the Year; inducted into Pro Football Hall of Fame in 1998

TEAMS: Chicago Bears 1981–1992

HEAD COACH TEAMS: San Francisco 49ers 2009–10

CAREER STATS

	Interceptions	Sacks	Tackles	Fumbles
G	INT	TOTAL	TOTAL	REC
179	7	19	1,488	12

COACHING RECORD

Regular Season	
WINS	LOSSES
18	22

Instead of choosing a former coach or teammate to present him at his Hall of Fame induction, Mike Singletary chose his wife, Kim. She is the only wife ever to deliver an introductory speech at the ceremonies.

Mike Singletary established himself as one of the greatest middle linebackers in NFL history during a distinguished twelve-year career with the Chicago Bears. He was the anchor of the fearsome Bears defense nicknamed the "Monsters of the Midway" and helped the team win its first Super Bowl title in 1985. Singletary intimidated opponents with his glaring eyes and was known for his focus and intensity on the playing field. He was the son of a preacher and is an ordained minister.

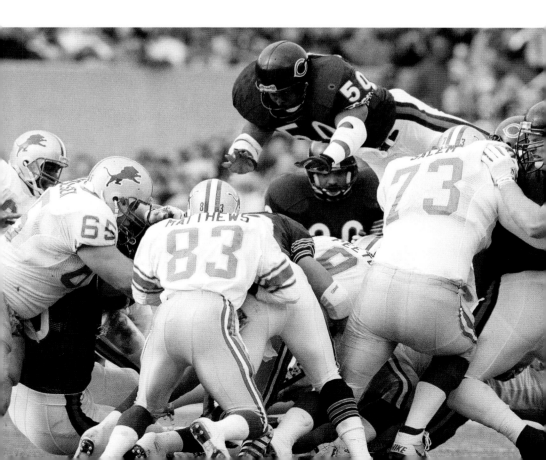

BRAD SMITH

My faith is everything to me. It's the foundation for how I live and view life. Growing up, my family and I went through a lot of adversity, and that helped us build a special bond. My family has kept me grounded and shown amazing support. They show real love. They have helped me to see that, next to being a great husband to my wife, being a great father to my children is the most important job I have in life. The people in my family have been living examples of this passage, and seeing them happy is extremely important to me.

As a young kid growing up, the coaches for the Little League football team I played on required us to memorize a scripture passage each week. Once we did, we had to recite that passage at practice. So this passage from Hebrews was the first one we learned, and it had a remarkable effect on my life. It was my first encounter with "real life" faith. To start memorizing a Bible verse as a seven-year-old was a little tough. Having to get up in front of everyone and say it out loud was scary. But as the scripture states, "Faith is the substance of things hoped for. . ." I had hope that God was with me and that He would give me strength to accomplish this task, and He did. This lesson has stayed with me my entire life.

When we are faced with situations in our lives where there seems to be no trace of God, faith will be our evidence that He is with us.

BRAD SMITH

POSITION: Wide receiver   **WEIGHT**: 213 lbs

HEIGHT: 6 foot 2   **NUMBER**: 16

BORN: December 12, 1983, in Youngstown, Ohio

HIGH SCHOOL: Chaney

COLLEGE: Missouri

DRAFTED: Fourth round (103rd overall) by the New York Jets in 2006

HONORS: Hula Bowl MVP 2006

TEAMS: New York Jets 2006-10; Buffalo Bills 2011-12; Philadelphia Eagles 2013-2014

CAREER STATS

	Receiving				KO Ret			
G	REC	YDS	AVG	TD	TOTAL	YDS	AVG	TD
127	104	987	9.5	5	112	2,873	25.7	4

Passing							Rushing			
COMP	ATT	%	YDS	TD	INT	RAT	ATT	YDS	TD	AVG
4	10	40.0	51	1	2	50.4	134	972	4	7.3

Brad Smith is a versatile athlete who is the only player in NFL history to score touchdowns by kickoff returns (four), receptions (five), rushing (four), passing (one), and blocked punt (twice). Smith played quarterback at Missouri and holds several school, Big 12 Conference, and NCAA Division-I records. He was the first player to pass for 8,000 yards and run for 4,000 yards in his career and the first to pass for 2,000 yards and run for 1,000 yards in a season twice in a career. He has been primarily a special teams player and wide receiver in the NFL. Smith's 106-yard kickoff return for a touchdown against the Indianapolis Colts on December 27, 2009, is the longest play in Jets history.

EMMITT SMITH

Trust in the LORD with all your heart and lean not on your own understanding; in all your ways submit to him, and he will make your paths straight.

PROVERBS 3:5–6

I grew up imagining what it would be like to play football like Jim Brown, Tony Dorsett, Walter Payton. . . My dream as a little boy was to play for the Dallas Cowboys. But in high school, I was told I didn't have the size or speed to even make it in college. It bothered me to hear people discredit my ability. I used it as fuel, as motivation, and it kept me going and striving to be successful because those critics didn't hold my destiny in their hands.

I ended up getting a scholarship to the University of Florida in 1987, and before I went, my grandmother told me to read this verse from Proverbs.

From then on, whenever I found myself in a difficult situation, I would lean on this verse. My dream became a reality when I was drafted by the Cowboys. After that, I allowed my faith to take a backseat. I was partying in clubs and doing all the wrong things. But at one point, I had to ask myself, "What am I doing?" My spirit was churning. I started thirsting for the Lord. I was going through turbulence in my career, and the only thing I knew was to trust in the Lord.

I ran into Pastor T. D. Jakes shortly afterward, and it all changed. Faith became my number one priority.

My Lord and Savior Jesus Christ gave me the passion and love for whatever it is I wanted to do. He showed me I can do whatever I want to do if I keep Him first. I can walk around with confidence knowing God has my back. I can walk around with confidence believing that He has purposed my life for greatness, not just in football, but for helping others. God Almighty has the final say where you go. If you trust in Him with all your heart and lean not on your own understanding and allow Him to direct your path, you will be successful. But you have to do your part.

EMMITT SMITH

POSITION: Running back

WEIGHT: 221 lbs

HEIGHT: 5 foot 9

NUMBER: 22

BORN: May 15, 1969, in Pensacola, Florida

HIGH SCHOOL: Escambia

COLLEGE: Florida

DRAFTED: First round (17th overall) by the Dallas Cowboys in 1990

HONORS: Inducted into Pro Football Hall of Fame in 2010; eight-time Pro Bowler; four-time first-team All-Pro; 1990 NFL Associated Press Offensive Rookie of the Year; 1993 NFL Associated Press Most Valuable Player; 1993 Bert Bell Award for NFL Player of the Year by the Maxwell Club; 1993 NFL Super Bowl MVP

TEAMS: Dallas Cowboys 1990–2002; Arizona Cardinals 2003–04

CAREER STATS

	Rushing				Receiving			
G	ATT	YDS	AVG	TD	REC	YDS	AVG	TD
224	4,409	18,355	4.2	164	515	3,224	6.3	11

Considered too small and too slow by many major college recruiters, Emmitt Smith proved the skeptics were wrong. He was an All-American at Florida and went on to become the NFL's all-time leading rusher, surpassing Walter Payton's career record. Smith helped the Dallas Cowboys win three Super Bowl championships. Smith won four rushing titles, led the league in rushing touchdowns four times, and is the all-time leader with 164 rushing touchdowns. Smith is the only running back to ever win a Super Bowl, the NFL MVP award, the NFL rushing crown, and the Super Bowl MVP award in the same season (1993). He's a member of the Cowboys Ring of Honor and was inducted into the Pro Football Hall of Fame in 2010. Smith briefly worked as an analyst after his retirement.

MATT STOVER

He has shown you, O mortal, what is good. And what does the LORD require of you? To act justly and to love mercy and to walk humbly with your God.

MICAH 6:8

There are a lot of verses in the Bible that I love, but I love to be guided and directed to know exactly what is required of me.

As an athlete, you know what's required out of you from your coach, from your team, from your trainers. Whatever your role is, however it's been defined, you know you can work within those limitations, and that empowers you to be the player and person that you should be. In this verse, the prophet Micah talks about what the Lord requires from you.

The first thing is to act justly. In this world there's so much injustice that I know that if I can act justly and treat people with honor and respect as God's creation, God will be pleased by that.

The second is to love mercy. How much mercy do we need in our lifetime? There are many times when we need to be forgiven or we need to have mercy on someone else or on ourselves, so I know that I love mercy. I'm not a perfect person myself, and therefore, I'm going to show mercy and I'm going to love it. That's something that's so contradictory in our world because we live in a vindictive culture. Yet God requires that we show mercy.

The third is to walk humbly. Well in this culture, humility is not valued very highly. It's more about self-righteousness, about "I can do this. I can do that." Instead, I try to think, *How can the Lord work through me?* and *Thank You, Lord, for my abilities.* I'm so thankful that He used me as an athlete to play the game of football. He gave me the strength and the knowledge to be able to do it, and I am so thankful He gave me that blessing.

MATT STOVER

POSITION: Kicker

KICKED: Right

HEIGHT: 5 foot 11

NUMBER: 3

WEIGHT: 178 lbs

BORN: January 27, 1968, in Dallas, Texas

HIGH SCHOOL: Lake Highlands

COLLEGE: Louisiana Tech

DRAFTED: Twelfth round (329th overall) by the New York Giants in 1990

HONORS: One-time Pro Bowler; one-time first-team All-Pro

TEAMS: New York Giants 1990; Cleveland Browns 1991–95; Baltimore Ravens 1996–2008; Indianapolis Colts 2009

CAREER STATS

	Ranges					
G	0-19	20-29	30-39	40-49	50+	PTS
297	14-15	170-173	146-162	128-181	13-32	2,004

Pat.			Field Goals			
XPM	XPA	%	FGM	FGA	%	LNG
591	594	99.5	471	563	83.7	55

Stover threw an interception on a fake field goal in his only career passing attempt with Cleveland in 1992.

Matt Stover was one of the NFL's most accurate kickers during a twenty-year career in the NFL. He led the league with thirty-one successful field goals in 2000 and finished in the top 3 five times. Stover spent his rookie season on injured reserve with the New York Giants, who won the Super Bowl that year. He joined the Cleveland Browns the following year and spent nearly all of his career with the franchise, which moved to Baltimore in 1996 and became the Ravens. Stover recorded all of the Ravens' points during a five-game stretch in 2000 in which the offense didn't score a touchdown. He kicked two field goals and four extra points in Baltimore's win over the Giants in the Super Bowl that season. Stover had eighteen game-winning field goals in his career. His last game was the 2009 Super Bowl with Indianapolis, a loss to New Orleans. Stover was the oldest player in Super Bowl history at age forty-two.

RYAN SUCCOP

*The Lord is near. Do not be anxious about anything,
but in every situation, by prayer and petition,
with thanksgiving, present your requests to God.
And the peace of God, which transcends all understanding,
will guard your hearts and your minds in Christ Jesus.*

PHILIPPIANS 4:5–7

These verses are very important to me because I think a lot of times in our world—whether we're in a high-pressure environment like the NFL or just dealing with the struggles of life in general—we tend to spend our time worrying. And when we do that, we're basically saying that we don't trust God.

That's not what God wants us to do. He wants us not to worry, and He tells us right here in scripture. Whatever your trouble, God says, don't worry about it. Instead, pray about it. And let the peace of God, which transcends any understanding that humans can have, let that come over you instead of worrying.

This verse has always kind of stuck close to me. I actually read it before every game so that I can go on the field and relax and say to myself, "Hey, I've got nothing to worry about. I can go out and be free. I can play free." That is something that's always helped me.

Being a place kicker in the NFL comes with its own set of stresses. It happens all the time—many games are decided by a last-second field goal. To the outside observer, this could be perceived as a high-stress, high-worry situation. And many times, it is. But when I think about this verse in scripture, it frees me up to do what I need to do on the field. Whenever I'm in that situation, I know that the only way to find peace is in giving up my worry to God.

RYAN SUCCOP

POSITION: Kicker

KICKED: Right

HEIGHT: 6 foot 2

NUMBER: 8

WEIGHT: 215 lbs

BORN: September 19, 1986, in Pittsburgh, Pennsylvania

HIGH SCHOOL: Tates Creek

COLLEGE: South Carolina

DRAFTED: Seventh round (256th overall) by the Kansas City Chiefs in 2009

HONORS: Two-time nominee for the Lou Groza Award given to the top placekicker in NCAA; 2007 nominee for the Ray Guy Award for top punter in NCAA; 2009 NFL All-Rookie Team

TEAMS: Kansas City Chiefs 2009–13; Tennessee Titans 2014–

CAREER STATS

	Ranges					
G	0-19	20-29	30-39	40-49	50+	PTS
96	1-1	38-39	48-55	40-55	11-19	601

Pat.			Field Goals			
XPM	XPA	%	FGM	FGA	%	LNG
187	187	100	138	169	81.7	54

Though he was often teased because his last name is pronounced "Suck-up," he said he never got into a fight over it.

Ryan Succop kicked and punted for three seasons at South Carolina before the Kansas City Chiefs selected him with the final pick in the 2009 draft. Despite being tagged with the "Mr. Irrelevant" title that goes to the last guy drafted each season, Succop had an outstanding rookie season. He tied an NFL record for highest field-goal percentage by a rookie in a season with 86.2 percent. He also passed NFL Hall of Famer Jan Stenerud for most field goals made by a rookie in Chiefs' history. Succop scored more points (104) than any other rookie in the NFL that year and was named to the All-Rookie team. He had a streak of twenty-one consecutive field goals in 2011 and kicked six field goals in a victory over the New Orleans Saints on September 23, 2012. Succop was released by the Chiefs after five seasons and signed with the Titans in 2014.

TIM TEBOW

For God so loved the world that he gave his one and only Son, that whoever believes in him shall not perish but have eternal life.

JOHN 3:16

This verse changed my life when I was a little boy. It's the essence of what I believe. It's an amazing verse that has the power to change lives. When I leave this world, I want to leave something behind that keeps on making a difference in people's lives. God wants us to make a difference in the world—in the lives of our family, friends, coaches, and teachers. The most important acts will live on forever, even after we are no longer on this earth. God wants us to do things that will have an impact. I want to leave behind a life in which I always tried to do things the right way. Most importantly, I want to act in a way that causes the people I help to want to help others.

TIM TEBOW

POSITION: Quarterback

HEIGHT: 6 foot 2

NUMBER: 15

WEIGHT: 236 lbs

THROWS: Left

BORN: August 14, 1987, in Makati City, Philippines

HIGH SCHOOL: Allen D. Nease

COLLEGE: Florida

DRAFTED: First round (25th overall) by the Denver Broncos in 2010

HONORS: 2007 Heisman Trophy winner; 2007 Associated College Football Player of the Year; 2007 and 2008 Maxwell Award winner

TEAMS: Denver Broncos 2010–2011; New York Jets 2012; Philadephia Eagles 2015–

CAREER STATS

	Passing								Rushing			
G	COMP	ATT	%	YDS	TD	INT	RAT		ATT	YDS	TD	AVG
35	173	361	47.9	2,422	17	9	75.3		197	989	12	5.0

Known as much for his public display of his Christian faith as his quarterback skills, Tim Tebow remains one of the most popular athletes in sports despite not playing in the NFL in 2013 and 2014. He was the first college sophomore to win a Heisman Trophy and led Florida to a national championship before going to the Denver Broncos. He became the starting quarterback in the sixth game of his second season and helped lead the Broncos to the playoffs. He threw the winning touchdown pass in an overtime win against Pittsburgh in the playoffs and finished the game with 316 yards passing. Despite his success and popularity, Tebow was traded to the New York Jets in the offseason after Denver signed Peyton Manning. Tebow didn't play much with the Jets in 2012, spent training camp with the New England Patriots in 2013, and worked as a college football analyst for ESPN before signing a one-year contract with the Philadelphia Eagles on April 20, 2015.

CEDRIC THORNTON

*"I am the vine; you are the branches.
If you remain in me and I in you, you will bear much fruit;
apart from me you can do nothing."*

JOHN 15:5

My father is a pastor and my mom is a minister, and I've been raised up to know that it's by no coincidence that I'm here. It's not by accident that I'm an NFL player. God put me in this situation. So everything I do, I try to glorify God; and every day out here on the football field, I give my all to please God because if I don't, then I'm telling Him I don't rely on Him and I don't depend on Him. That's a different motivation, a different mentality, and it helps me when I step on the field. I try to live the life God wants me to live. God put me in a position to put Him—not me—on a pedestal and to let everybody else know that if I can make it with God's help, they can make it, too. Whatever they want to do, they can do it.

I like this verse because it says I can do all things with God, but away from Him, I can't do anything. It's just a relief when you are not dependent on yourself and you know God provided you with your physical attributes and your characteristics, and if you just believe in Him, He will give you the strength of Samson and the courage of David to attack the giants in your life. It's a reminder that there's a greater person in control of you and your destiny.

EXTRA POINT

Thornton aspired to be a baseball or basketball player when he was a kid, but quickly realized he was too aggressive to play either sport. Football suited his personality better.

CEDRIC THORNTON

POSITION: Defensive end

WEIGHT: 309 lbs

HEIGHT: 6 foot 4

NUMBER: 72

BORN: June 21, 1988, in Star City, Arkansas

HIGH SCHOOL: Star City

COLLEGE: Southern Arkansas

DRAFTED: Signed as a rookie free agent by the Philadelphia Eagles in 2011

HONORS: First-team Little All-America 2009

TEAMS: Philadelphia Eagles 2011–

CAREER STATS

	Interceptions		Sacks	Tackles	Fumbles		
G	INT	IntTD	TOTAL	TOTAL	FRCD	REC	TD
48	0	0	3	103	1	3	1

Cedric Thornton was a two-year starter at Division II Southern Arkansas before he became the fifth player from the small school to reach the NFL. After spending most of his first season on the practice squad, Thornton became a key member of the defensive line rotation in 2012. He developed into one of the league's best run-stopping linemen in 2013 and started every game over the next two seasons. Thornton's first career sack came against Atlanta's Matt Ryan, and the next was on Denver's Peyton Manning. Thornton recovered a fumble in the end zone for a touchdown in a win over St. Louis on October 5, 2014. He nearly scored on another fumble return in that game, but was tackled after running 40 yards.

DAVID TYREE

To the weak I became weak, to win the weak.
I have become all things to all people so that
by all possible means I might save some.

1 CORINTHIANS 9:22

This verse is one of the first scriptures that stuck in my soul as a young believer. In it, Paul is teaching his readers to serve all who may believe. This verse shows the length to which Paul was willing to go to, the humility Paul exhibited so that the gospel would be advanced, so that souls would be saved, so that people would come to the knowledge of a tremendous Savior, Christ Jesus.

"I have become all things to all people" is a part I really love. Paul didn't conform to others' behavior; he didn't lower his standards. But he did want to demonstrate humility in identifying with others, witnessing to Christ by bearing the sin and the burden and the challenges of others. Whatever it took to be able to show Christ to another, Paul was willing to do it.

This verse really spoke to me a long time ago about what being a Christian is all about. It quickened my soul and helped me aspire to a greater measure of service and humility.

As a professional athlete, you have a platform. As a Christian, it can be dangerous in some ways because you know you have a sense of duty and responsibility, but right alongside it there's a cunning sense of people who propel you to kind of call that platform sort of a pedestal. So there's a sense of, "I've been noticed, I've been esteemed." But it's not for the right reasons you've been esteemed, so you have to be intentional about the act of humility. As much as it's a grace from God, it has to be an intentional decision to submit yourself for the sake that somebody will see Christ in your service and be strengthened by it.

EXTRA POINT

In 2006, Tyree and his wife, Leilah, started Next in Line, a project that counsels teenagers.

DAVID TYREE

POSITION: Wide receiver

WEIGHT: 205 lbs

HEIGHT: 6 foot

NUMBER: 85

BORN: January 3, 1980, in Livingston, New Jersey

HIGH SCHOOL: Montclair

COLLEGE: Syracuse

DRAFTED: Sixth round (211th overall) by the New York Giants in 2003

HONORS: One-time Pro Bowler

TEAMS: New York Giants 2003–07; Baltimore Ravens 2008

CAREER STATS

| | Receiving | | | |
G	REC	YDS	AVG	TD
83	54	650	12	4

David Tyree caught only fifty-four passes in six seasons in the NFL with the New York Giants and Baltimore Ravens, but his final reception is widely considered the greatest play in Super Bowl history. Tyree made an acrobatic, one-handed catch, clutching the ball against his helmet as he fell backward to the turf during the winning drive in the final minutes to help the Giants beat the previously unbeaten New England Patriots 17–14 in the Super Bowl on February 3, 2008. Tyree was selected for the Pro Bowl in 2005 for his performance as a special teams player. Tyree was hired by the Giants in 2014 to be the director of player personnel.

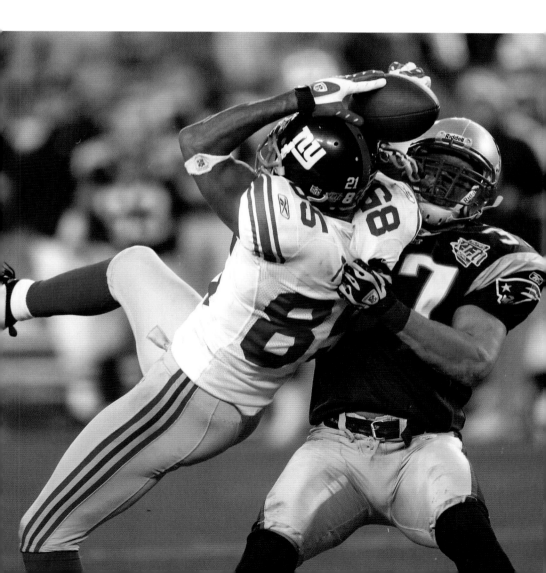

JULIAN VANDERVELDE

For the Spirit God gave us does not make us timid,
but gives us power, love and self-discipline.

2 TIMOTHY 1:7

I feel that this verse encompasses everything it takes to be successful, everything that it takes to preach the Word of God, to minister to others, and be a man of God. The thing that holds us back from doing what God wants us to do is fear—fear that we can't do something and fear that we're not good enough. If we let fear control us, we're never going to accomplish much because we're always going to be afraid of failure.

But God gives us power. He gives us power to speak—power to stand up to those who try to knock us down. When we love others in His power, they are more likely to listen to us; we can then help them on the road they're trying to walk, and they can help us in return.

It's that self-discipline from the Spirit that's so important, especially today when we are being pulled in so many different directions. In a world driven by marketing and materialism, that self-discipline helps us to be able to look beyond the world's influence, examine our goals, and have faith that God's direction for life will help us to stay on track.

Because we don't get a lot of chances on Sunday to go to church, Bible study really helps me to be disciplined during the season. We have chapel service the night before games, and between that and Bible study, I'm getting together with like-minded people, I'm discussing ideas, and I'm getting into the Word. I find what helps me is to take a lesson from each of those sessions and try to apply it each week.

Love is the most important thing. We're called to love others as God loves us, and there is no greater calling, no more powerful force than that.

Vandervelde earned a double major in English and Religious studies and a minor in Japanese at Iowa. He hopes to one day move to Nagasaki, Japan, to help rebuild the Christian community.

JULIAN VANDERVELDE

POSITION: Offensive lineman

WEIGHT: 300 lbs

HEIGHT: 6 foot 2

NUMBER: 61

BORN: October 7, 1987, in Davenport, Iowa

HIGH SCHOOL: William M. Raines

COLLEGE: Central

DRAFTED: Fifth round (161st overall) by the Philadelphia Eagles in 2011

HONORS: Second-team All-Big Ten 2010

TEAMS: Philadelphia Eagles 2011–

CAREER STATS

G
16

A four-year letterman at Iowa, Julian Vandervelde is a versatile lineman and valued backup at guard and center. Vandervelde has several talents beyond the football field. He began singing in the choir in first grade and was part of a group that sang the National Anthem for President Barack Obama in 2010 and Bill and Hillary Clinton in 2008. Vandervelde also is the owner of the Quad City WolfPack, a minor league team in the Midwest Football Alliance.

MICHAEL VICK

*I called out to the LORD,
out of my distress, and he answered me.*

JONAH 2:2 ESV

I was always a believer growing up, but when you are young, you feel like you know it all; and when it seems you have everything like fame and money, at that particular time in your life, you can stray. Looking back when you are older, you realize you were still a kid. I've done a lot of sinning in my life. I'm not a saint. I'm no different than anyone else. But as I ask for forgiveness, I continue to receive blessings. I'm so blessed to be where I am right now, and it took me falling down, hitting the bottom, to get back up again. Before I was incarcerated, it was all about me. When I got to prison, I realized I couldn't do it anymore. The one thing I could rely on was my faith in God. Through the unfortunate situation I put myself in, I found Jesus and asked Him for forgiveness and turned my life over to God.

There were a lot of Bible verses that helped me in that time, especially the book of Jeremiah. But this was the one passage that stands out. Jonah was cast deep into the sea and swallowed up by a fish. But he called out to the Lord, and he was saved. I was cast aside too, sitting in a prison cell, swallowed up by the mistakes I had made and the culture I grew up in. But I reached out for Jesus, and I was saved. Being in that moment, being in that situation, was so surreal because I knew what I had done really didn't matter anymore. Now I'm more at peace. God has taken over my life. I don't have to worry about being dynamic or anything. God is in control of that.

MICHAEL VICK

POSITION: Quarterback

THROWS: Left

HEIGHT: 6 foot

NUMBER: 7

WEIGHT: 215 lbs

BORN: July 26, 1980, in Newport News, Virginia

HIGH SCHOOL: Warwick

COLLEGE: Virginia Tech

DRAFTED: First round (1st overall) by the Atlanta Falcons in 2001

HONORS: Four-time Pro Bowl pick; Associated Press Comeback Player of the Year 2010

TEAMS: Atlanta Falcons 2001–06; Philadelphia Eagles 2009–13; New York Jets 2014–

CAREER STATS

	Passing								Rushing			
G	COMP	ATT	%	YDS	TD	INT	RAT	ATT	YDS	TD	AVG
138	1,767	3,151	56.1	22,293	131	87	80.4	853	6,010	36	7.0

One of the most talented athletes to play quarterback, Michael Vick has run for more yards than any player to ever play the position in the NFL. He left Virginia Tech after his sophomore season and helped the Atlanta Falcons become the first team to beat the Green Bay Packers in a playoff game at Lambeau Field in just his second year in the league. Vick guided the Falcons to the NFC championship game in 2004 but missed two seasons after he was imprisoned for running a dog-fighting operation. Vick returned to the NFL with the Philadelphia Eagles and emerged as a team leader, inspirational player, and had his best all-around season passing in 2010. Vick spent five seasons with the Eagles before joining the New York Jets in 2014.

TROY VINCENT

*And we know that in all things God works for
the good of those who love him,
who have been called according to his purpose.*

ROMANS 8:28

I send this verse out fifty to sixty times a day in my text messages and e-mails. Someone asks how I'm doing. My response is Romans 8:28. Someone says, "Hey man, I just lost my job or I got laid off." I give them Romans 8:28. Why? Because *all* things work together for the good of those who love the Lord: *all* things. This verse gives us what we need to keep believing and keep pushing because *all* things work together. Life may seem tough now. Circumstances may be working against you. People may be speaking ill about you. But you keep pressing, you keep challenging God on His Word, and you keep believing because *all* things work together for good when you love the Lord.

Because I love the Lord, I'm being led by Him. I'm that follower. My everyday existence is because of Him. So when I look at that scripture, if I'm doing what I'm supposed to be doing by the will of God, then God will do His work. Because at the end of the day, God also says He's the beginning and the end. He's the Alpha and the Omega, so God knows my thoughts before I even think them. This is why I can live by these good habits in trusting Christ. It is through the love of Christ and me being His child and following His will and not mine that all things are going to work together. That's when I feel I'm in God's hands.

When I share that scripture with others and they ask me what it means, I tell them that it means we have to believe; we have to keep exercising our faith. And don't just say it—do it. God doesn't want us to be just hearers of His Word. He wants us to be doers—to know what He wants and then act on it with the confidence that God is always at work.

Vincent shares the record for the longest interception in Eagles history. On November 4, 1996, against the Dallas Cowboys, James Willis intercepted Troy Aikman's pass four yards deep into the end zone. Willis ran fourteen yards before lateraling to Vincent, who returned the interception ninety yards for a 104-yard touchdown to seal a 31–21 win.

TROY VINCENT

POSITION: Cornerback

WEIGHT: 200 lbs

HEIGHT: 6 foot 1

NUMBER: 23

BORN: June 8, 1970, in Trenton, New Jersey

HIGH SCHOOL: Pennsbury

COLLEGE: Wisconsin

DRAFTED: First round (7th overall) by the Miami Dolphins in 1992

HONORS: Five-time Pro Bowler; one-time first-team All-Pro

TEAMS: Miami Dolphins 1992–95; Philadelphia Eagles 1996–2003; Buffalo Bills 2004–06; Washington Redskins 2006

CAREER STATS

	Interceptions		Sacks	Tackles	Fumbles	
G	INT	IntTD	TOTAL	TOTAL	FRCD	REC
207	47	3	5.5	738	12	12

Troy Vincent was one of the NFL's best cornerbacks for a decade from the mid-1990s to mid-2000s. He led the NFL in interceptions with seven in 1999. Vincent was named to the Philadelphia Eagles Seventy-Fifth Anniversary Team in 2007 and entered the franchise's Hall of Fame in 2012. Vincent served as a team captain for thirteen of his fifteen seasons and was president of the NFL Players' Association from 2004 to 2008. Vincent became the NFL's vice president of active player development in February 2010. He was named executive vice president of football operations by NFL Commissioner Roger Goodell in March 2014. Vincent was the 2002 winner of the Walter Payton NFL Man of the Year Award for his outstanding community service.

KURT WARNER

Work willingly at whatever you do,
as though you were working for the Lord rather than for people.

COLOSSIANS 3:23 NLT

Any time you mention Jesus or faith around the football field, people are turned off. I think it scares a lot of people. When you stand up and say, "Thank You, Jesus," they think you are saying, "Thank You for being here. Thank You for moving my arm forward and making the ball go into that guy's hands so that we could score a touchdown and win the game."

But in essence, it's a matter of thanking Him for the opportunity, thanking Him for being there in my life, for being the stronghold, for being the focus and the strength to accomplish all things, to accomplish anything, and to be where I am at, to have gone through everything I have gone through. It's a constant thing in my life. It's not just for something specific He did on the football field to help us win; it's for everything that He has done in my life up to that point and for everything He will continue to do in my life from here until eternity.

But I don't have to stand on my chair with a Bible and yell out scripture verses or condemn people for being sinners to have influence on them. By understanding what my priorities are and never wavering, by living like this verse says, that's how you influence people. It's about living your life with a certain sense of excellence. And when people start to scratch their heads and wonder what it is that makes me different, that's when I tell them the answer is Jesus. And then I let Him do the hard work.

KURT WARNER

POSITION: Quarterback

THROWS: Right

HEIGHT: 6 foot 2

NUMBER: 13

WEIGHT: 220 lbs

BORN: June 22, 1971, in Burlington, Iowa

HIGH SCHOOL: Regis

COLLEGE: Northern Iowa

DRAFTED: Undrafted

HONORS: Four-time Pro Bowler; two-time first-team All-Pro; two-time Associated Press NFL Most Valuable Player; 1999 Super Bowl MVP; 1999 Bert Bell Award for NFL Player of the Year by the Maxwell Club

TEAMS: St. Louis Rams 1998–2003; New York Giants 2004; Arizona Cardinals 2005–09

CAREER STATS

	Passing						
G	COMP	ATT	%	YDS	TD	INT	RAT
125	2,666	4,070	65.5	32,344	208	128	93.7

Kurt Warner is widely considered the best undrafted player in NFL history. He was signed as a rookie free agent by the Green Bay Packers in 1994 but didn't make the team. He worked at a grocery store, stocking shelves for minimum wage and also played in the Arena Football League before the Rams gave him a chance in the NFL. Warner spent his first season as the third-string quarterback and became the starter in 1999 after Trent Green injured his knee in the preseason. Warner combined with Marshall Faulk, Isaac Bruce, and Torry Holt to form an offense nicknamed "The Greatest Show on Turf" while leading the Rams to the franchise's first Super Bowl title. He helped the Rams' offense register three straight five hundred–point seasons, an NFL record. Warner later led the Arizona Cardinals to their first Super Bowl, a loss to the Pittsburgh Steelers on February 1, 2009. Craig Morton and Peyton Manning are the only other quarterbacks to start for two teams in the Super Bowl. Warner holds several NFL records and has posted the third-highest passing yards in Super Bowl history. Warner joined the NFL Network as an analyst in 2010.

CARY WILLIAMS

The LORD is my light and my salvation— whom shall I fear? The LORD is the stronghold of my life—of whom shall I be afraid.

PSALM 27:1

As a guy who came from a small school (Division II Washburn University), being picked 229th in the 2008 NFL draft, getting cut twice, and spending more than a year on the practice squad, it's been an uphill battle for me since I entered the league. It's almost like the David and Goliath story. I had to have faith and understand that God had something great out there for me. In my position, being a cornerback, I go up against a lot of big-name wide receivers, guys who are future Hall of Famers. In those situations, I can't be fearful. I have to go out there and play. This Bible verse speaks to me every day. Each time I line up, I think about this verse. I think about going out there and making plays and playing the way God has gifted me with my abilities.

The Lord is my light and salvation, so I have no fear. I don't walk around with fear of losing my life. I don't worry about negative things, and I make sure I'm ready if it's my time. I don't put myself in certain situations. I don't drink. I don't go to nightclubs. If I'm doing the right things, I feel good things will happen for me. Faith is important for me, my wife, and my daughter. My grandma always prayed and taught me to believe in Jesus Christ. Then my cousin adopted me and got me involved in the church, and I became saved. Once I gave my life to Christ, my life began to change. I'm not the most perfect human being. But through Christ, we can all change and do all things.

EXTRA POINT

Williams returned the first interception of his career 63 yards for a touchdown against Cleveland on September 27, 2012.

CARY WILLIAMS

POSITION: Cornerback

WEIGHT: 185 lbs

HEIGHT: 6 foot 1

NUMBER: 26

BORN: December 23, 1984, in Miami, Florida

HIGH SCHOOL: Chaminade-Madonna

COLLEGE: Washburn

DRAFTED: Seventh round (229th overall) by the Tennessee Titans in 2008

HONORS: Super Bowl champion 2012

TEAMS: Tennessee Titans 2008–09; Baltimore Ravens 2009–12; Philadelphia Eagles 2013–14; Seattle Seahawks 2015–

CAREER STATS

	Interceptions		Sacks	Tackles	Fumbles		
G	INT	IntTD	TOTAL	TOTAL	FRCD	REC	TD
87	9	1	2	258	4	1	0

Cary Williams overcame a difficult childhood and took an unconventional road to the NFL through a Division II college program. He developed into a physical, playmaking cornerback who played a key role in helping the Ravens win the Super Bowl in 2012. Williams intercepted two passes during Baltimore's playoff run, including one pick to seal a victory over Tom Brady and the New England Patriots in the AFC championship game. Williams signed a free-agent contract with the Eagles in 2013 and started every game in his first two seasons.

RUSSELL WILSON

*Seek the Kingdom of God above all else, and live righteously,
and he will give you everything you need.*

MATTHEW 6:33 NLT

I chose the number three for my jersey with the Seattle Seahawks to honor the Holy Trinity: the Father, the Son, and the Holy Spirit. Faith has always been the foundation for my family. My father passed away a day after I was drafted by Colorado in the Major League Baseball draft, but first he heard me tell him the good news at the hospital before he went in peace. That's how I knew the Lord was real.

God is so good. I'm a shorter quarterback, slightly under five foot eleven. Everybody said I wouldn't be able to play in the NFL. God doesn't care about naysayers. He prepared me, and nobody can stop you when you believe in Him, like this verse says, and you are blessed by Him. I'm always asked if I'm nervous before games, but I'm never nervous. I don't have highs and lows because I play for Him. I have no nerves.

I truly believe God gave me a tremendous gift, and I'm trying to use it to the best of my ability and give honor to Jesus and give Him all the glory because I wouldn't be where I am without Him. I tweet Bible verses every day. You have to stand for something, and He has given me this tremendous platform.

My teammates and I always talk about playing for an audience of one. It doesn't matter if there are ninety thousand people in the stands and two million viewers watching at home. It doesn't matter what the critics say, whether they say how good you are or how bad you are. It's all about God. You have to give Him all the glory. He has something so amazing for you in His plans that you can't even see it yet.

RUSSELL WILSON

POSITION: Quarterback

THROWS: Right

HEIGHT: 5 foot 11

NUMBER: 3

WEIGHT: 203 lbs

BORN: November 29, 1988, in Richmond, Virginia

HIGH SCHOOL: Collegiate State

COLLEGE: North Carolina State, Wisconsin

DRAFTED: Third round (75th overall) by the Seattle Seahawks in 2012

HONORS: Two-time Pro Bowl pick

TEAMS: Seattle Seahawks 2012–

CAREER STATS

	Passing							Rushing			
G	COMP	ATT	%	YDS	TD	INT	RAT	ATT	YDS	TD	AVG
48	794	1,252	63.4	9,950	72	26	98.6	308	1,877	11	6.1

Russell Wilson followed up an outstanding rookie season with the Seattle Seahawks by leading them to their first Super Bowl championship in franchise history in just his second year. Wilson and the Seahawks beat Peyton Manning and the Denver Broncos 43–8 to win Super Bowl XLVIII. Wilson set a rookie record with a 100.0 passer rating and tied Manning's rookie record with twenty-six touchdown passes in 2012. He tossed another twenty-six touchdown passes in 2013. Wilson had 20 to go with a career-best 3.475 yards passing in 2014 while leading the Seahawks to twelve wins and a second straight NFC West title. He nearly guided the Seahawks to a comeback win and their second straight Super Bowl championship, but threw an interception at the goal-line in the final minute against the New England Patriots. Wilson is also one of the best scrambling quarterbacks in the league and set a career-best with 849 yards rushing in 2014.

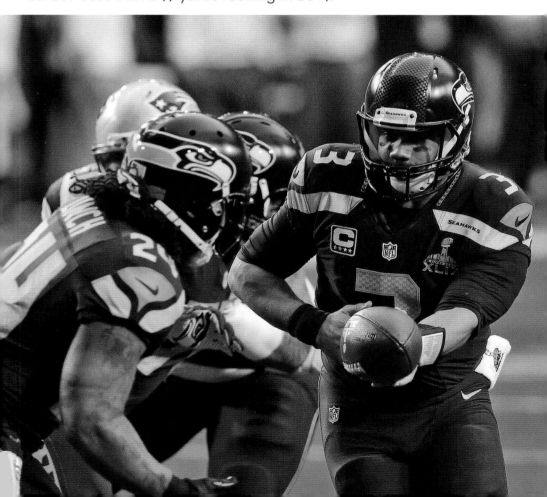

ABOUT THE AUTHOR

ROB MAADDI has been a Philadelphia sports writer for the Associated Press since 2000. He's covered the Super Bowl, World Series, NBA Finals, Stanley Cup Finals, and numerous major sporting events throughout his career.

Rob has coauthored three children's sports books and has written a biography on Mike Schmidt. A devoted Christian, Rob strives every day to make a difference and be a blessing. Rob is a missionary athlete with the Deacons Prison Ministry softball team. He visits inmates, shares his testimony, and preaches about Jesus Christ.

Rob, his wife, Remy, and their twin girls, Alexia and Melina, reside in South Jersey.

SCRIPTURE INDEX

Art Credit

10 Chris Park / AP Photo **13** Brian Garfinkel / AP Photo **14** Paul Spinelli / AP Photo **17** Paul Spinelli / AP Photo **18** Damian Strohmeyer / AP Photo **21** Scott Boehm / AP Photo **22** Brian Garfinkel / AP Photo **25** Paul Sakuma / AP Photo **26** Phelan M. Ebenhack / AP Photo **29** Rick Scuteri / AP Photo **30** Damian Strohmeyer / AP Photo **33** Michael Perez / AP Photo **34** Damian Strohmeyer / AP Photo **37** Matt Rourke / AP Photo **38** Jeff Haynes / AP Photo **41** Tony Dejak / AP Photo **42** Rogelio Solis / AP Photo **45** Don Wright / AP Photo **46** David Durochik/ AP Photo **49** Tom Olmscheid / AP Photo **50** Scott Boehm / AP Photo **53** Miles Kennedy / AP Photo **54** Matt Slocum / AP Photo **57** Reed Hoffmann / AP Photo **58** Vernon Biever / AP Photo **61** Al Golub / AP Photo **62** Paul Spinelli / AP Photo **65** Bill Kostroun / AP Photo **66** Damian Strohmeyer / AP Photo **69** Bill Kostroun / AP Photo **70** David Drapkin / AP Photo **73** David Drapkin / AP Photo **74** Paul Jasienski / AP Photo **77** Rick Scuteri / AP Photo **78** Scott Boehm / AP Photo **81** Charles Rex Arbogast / AP Photo **82** Evan Pinkus / AP Photo **85** Damian Strohmeyer / AP Photo **86** Kevin Terrell / AP Photo **89** James D Smith / AP Photo **90** David Durochik / AP Photo **93** NFL Photos / AP Photo **94** Tom Hauck / AP Photo **97** Don Wright / AP Photo **98** Paul Spinelli / AP Photo **101** Tom Hauck / AP Photo **102** Michael Zito / AP Photo **105** Tony Avelar / AP Photo **106** Michael Perez / AP Photo **109** Ben Margot / AP Photo **110** Damian Strohmeyer / AP Photo **113** Tom Hauck / AP Photo **114** Paul Jasienski / AP Photo **117** Brandon Wade / AP Photo **118** Paul Spinelli / AP Photo **121** Patrick Johnston / AP Photo **122** Tom DiPace / AP Photo **125** Darron Cummings / AP Photo **126** Greg Trott / AP Photo **129** Gene J. Puskar / AP Photo **130** Duane Burleson / AP Photo **133** Paul Sancya / AP Photo **134** Paul Jasienski / AP Photo **137** Charlie Riedel / AP Photo **138** Paul Jasienski / AP Photo **141** Denis Poroy / AP Photo **142** Scott Boehm / AP Photo **145** Matt Ludtke / AP Photo **146** Damian Strohmeyer / AP Photo **149** Brian Garfinkel / AP Photo **150** Damian Strohmeyer / AP Photo **153** Michael Perez / AP Photo **154** Tom DiPace / AP Photo **157** Kevin Reece / Icon Sportswire via AP Photo **158** Kevin Terrell / AP Photo **161** Ted S. Warren / AP Photo **162** Al Messerschmidt / AP Photo **165** AP Photo **166** Paul Jasienski / AP Photo **169** Bill Kostroun / AP Photo **170** David Stluka / AP Photo **173** Tim Sharp / AP Photo **174** Chris Gardner / AP Photo **177** Gary Tramontina / AP Photo **178** Ed Zurga / AP Photo **181** Paul Spinelli / AP Photo **182** Damian Strohmeyer / AP Photo **185** Julie Jacobson / AP Photo **186** Paul Spinelli / AP Photo **189** Ron Cortes / AP Photo **190** Scott Boehm / AP Photo **193** Paul Spinelli / AP Photo **194** David Drapkin / AP Photo **197** Brian Garfinkel / AP Photo **198** Michael Perez / AP Photo **201** David Drapkin / AP Photo **202** Athlon Archive / AP Photo **205** Lynne Sladky / AP Photo **206** Jeff Roberson / AP Photo **209** Andrew J. Cohoon / AP Photo **210** Paul Jasienski / AP Photo **213** Susan Walsh / AP Photo **214** Paul Spinelli / AP Photo **217** Brynn Anderson / AP Photo